W9-AER-533

BERNARD F. DUKORE

WHERE LAUGHTER STOPS

PINTER'S TRAGICOMEDY

A LITERARY FRONTIERS EDITION

UNIVERSITY OF MISSOURI PRESS

COLUMBIA & LONDON

ACKNOWLEDGMENTS

I would like to thank Margaret Mitchell Dukore and Pro-
fessor Charles A. Carpenter, who read early drafts of this essay
and made valuable suggestions.

For permission to quote from Harold Pinter's plays, I wish
to thank Harold Pinter, ACTAC (Theatrical and Cinematic) Ltd.;
Convent Garden Press Ltd. for quotations from *Monologue*; Eyre
Methuen Ltd. for quotations from *The Homecoming, Tea Party*,
and *No Man's Land*; and Grove Press Inc. for *The Homecoming*,
Copyright © 1965 and 1966 by Harold Pinter Ltd.; *The Birthday
Party*, Copyright © 1959 by Harold Pinter; *The Room*, Copyright
© 1960 by Harold Pinter; *A Slight Ache*, Copyright © 1961 by
Harold Pinter; *The Caretaker*, Copyright © 1960 by Theatre Pro-
motions, Ltd.; *The Dumb Waiter*, Copyright © 1960 by Harold
Pinter; *Tea Party*, Copyright © 1967 by H. Pinter Ltd., *The
Basement*, Copyright © 1967 by H. Pinter Ltd.; *No Man's Land*,
Copyright © 1975 by Harold Pinter, Ltd. All rights reserved;
The Collection, Copyright © 1962 by Harold Pinter; *Old Times*,
Copyright © 1971 by Harold Pinter Limited; and *The Lover*,
Copyright © 1963 by H. Pinter Ltd.

Library of Congress Cataloging in Publication Data

Dukore, Bernard Frank, 1931–
    Where laughter stops.

    (A Literary frontiers edition)
    1. Pinter, Harold, 1930–   —Criticism and inter-
pretation. I. Title
PR6066.I53Z635   822'.9'14   76–15990
ISBN 0–8262–0208–X

TO MARGI

IN his *Defense of Poesy*, Sir Philip Sidney deprecated tragicomedy as "mongrel." Pedigree notwithstanding, the breed proved popular. In *A Midsummer Night's Dream*, Shakespeare's Athenian Theseus, with a Roman standard of generic purity, compared the rude mechanicals' description of their play, "very tragical mirth," to hot ice, and he wondered whether the discordant mixture of the merry and the tragical might be made concordant. Chaff notwithstanding, Shakespeare in other plays was able, in Theseus's words, to "find the concord of this discord." In the Renaissance, and for a long time thereafter, mongrel tragicomedy usually meant a serious action, as in tragedy, with a happy ending, as in comedy; and/or a major tragic plot whose scenes alternated with those of a comic subplot; and/or a mixture of aristocratic personages, appropriate to tragedy, with humble characters, appropriate to comedy, who might but did not necessarily meet at the end of the play.

In modern drama, however, generic distinctions infrequently derive from social classes, and while predominantly tragic and predominantly comic scenes may still alternate, modern drama's tragicomic mixture is usually not so much a matter of such alternation as it is, to employ Bernard Shaw's phrase, "a chemical combination which [makes] the spectator laugh with one side of his mouth and cry with the other."[1] Subsequent descriptions of modern or post-Ibsenite tragicomedy harmonize with Shaw's, but they do not adequately provide a comprehensive definition of the nature

1. Letter to Archibald Henderson, March 8, 1918, quoted in Henderson, *Bernard Shaw: Playboy and Prophet* (New York: Appleton, 1932), p. 616.

and structure of the genre.[2] For this reason, I should like to attempt to construct a definition that would formulate a hypothesis about the nature and structural characteristics of this modern, mongrel genre and then test this hypothesis by applying it to the plays of one of our most important contemporary playwrights, Harold Pinter.[3]

* * *

If pressed for a distinction between tragedy and comedy, the layman would probably declare that tragedy ends with death, whereas comedy ends with marriage; that

2. "The humor . . . only deepens the horror," says Eric Bentley in his important *The Life of Drama* (New York: Atheneum, 1964), which contains one of the more useful discussions of modern tragicomedy, and Bentley adds that the humor "also deepens the 'defeatism' with a smile of acceptance" (p. 353). In another perceptive work, *Currents in Contemporary Drama* (Bloomington: Indiana University Press, 1969), Ruby Cohn observes, "The modern blend of tragicomedy . . . attempts a union of opposites that often leaves us more aware of the opposites than of the union" (p. 197). But, as Bentley and Cohn would be among the first to admit, their insights do not constitute a conclusive definition of the nature of modern tragicomedy. Nor do those of Karl S. Guthke, whose *Modern Tragicomedy* (New York: Random House, 1966) is probably the most systematic attempt to do so. Unfortunately, less than half of this frequently valuable book focuses on modern drama, it analyzes only one play in depth, and the tragicomic patterns Guthke attempts to establish (pp. 78–88) are either imprecise ("a character fit for tragedy [contrasted] with a world that distinctly belongs to the realm of comedy"), with examples that are not self-evident demonstrations (is *The Misanthrope* of Molière—hardly a modern work—"now almost universally held to be a tragicomic play"?), or are extremely difficult to apply to particular plays (of "a comic person bringing about tragic disaster for others," even Guthke admits, "there are no really successful tragicomedies conforming to this pattern").

3. For earlier explorations of this hypothesis, see my "Spherical Tragedies and Comedies with Corpses," *Modern Drama* 18 (September 1975): 291–315; "*Widowers' Houses*: A Question of Genre," *Modern Drama* 17 (March 1974): 27–32; and "*Krapp's Last Tape* as Tragicomedy," *Modern Drama* 15 (March 1973): 351–54.

tragedy makes you sad or shocks you, whereas comedy makes you laugh or smile. These distinctions—the one focusing on the play's outcome, the other on the audience's response—are not only essentially valid, they are crucial factors in the identification of dramatic genres, including tragicomedy. Traditionally, tragedy progresses from good fortune to bad, from happiness to unhappiness. Traditionally, comedy progresses from bad or moderately satisfactory fortune to good or better fortune, from unhappiness to happiness. The cardinal, distinguishing characteristics of modern tragicomedy revolve around a particular kind of plot progression and outcome and the response it evokes among audiences. In modern tragicomedy, the play does not necessarily move to a happy or unhappy conclusion, nor does it necessarily conclude as it began. Rather, it establishes a basic affinity to one of the two major genres, tragedy or comedy, but its development denies the exclusive characteristics of the tragic or comic genre with which it is primarily associated—characteristics of plot, audience response, or both—and its conclusion denies the exclusiveness of the type of change associated with that genre. If a tragicomedy is primarily associated with tragedy or if its end resembles that of tragedy ("unhappy"), then that conclusion carries none of the affirmation, redemption, or catharsis (according to any definition of the term) characteristic of tragedy; it reveals neither stature nor heroism; and it discloses no moral order. At the end of such a play, one might smile at the characters' folly, or one might, to return to Shaw's phrase, "laugh with one side of his mouth and cry with the other." If the play is primarily associated with comedy, however, or if its end resembles that of comedy ("happy"), then its conclusion freezes laughter or smiles, it carries discomfort rather than comfort, it contains a sardonic or grim quality that denies happiness, and it mocks the frequently festive culmination of comedy. Although death need not necessarily

3

terminate such a play, the life that continues may be worse than death, which could constitute relief.

*   *   *

"The old categories of comedy and tragedy and farce are irrelevant," says Harold Pinter,[4] who does not refer to his plays in these terms, but rather in terms of a tragicomic mixture—the close interweaving of comic and tragic in *The Caretaker*, for instance.[5] Among Pinter's infrequent comments on genre, one is particularly suggestive. On August 14, 1960, in London's *Sunday Times*, he called *The Caretaker* "funny, up to a point. Beyond that point it ceases to be funny, and it was because of that point that I wrote it."[6]

The movement of a funny play to a point where it is no longer funny—where the comic nature of its characteristics ceases to be comic, where the audience stops laughing, where the nonfunny dominates—this movement constitutes the progress, conclusion, and effect of Pinter's distinctive tragicomedies. These plays conform to the cardinal characteristics of modern tragicomedy; they deny the exclusiveness of the attributes of the comic genre with which they are primarily associated, the type of change and conclusion associated with that genre, and the response that genre normally evokes. Moreover, Pinter's tragicomedies not only begin in a comic manner and then reach a point where laughter stops, but from that point on, the sources of the noncomic are the same as those of the comic, and they deny the comic qualities they have established. These character-

4. Harold Pinter, "Writing for Myself," *The Twentieth Century* 169 (February 1961): 175.
5. *Sunday Times* (London), August 14, 1960, quoted in Martin Esslin, *The Peopled Wound: The Work of Harold Pinter* (Garden City, N.Y.: Doubleday Anchor, 1970), p. 45.
6. Ibid.

4

istics define the shape, structure, and unity of each of Pinter's tragicomedies and the unity of virtually the entire Pinter canon.[7] Not that each play conforms schematically to this simple formula. Rather, Pinter varies what is essentially a basic structure, for in some plays laughter stops briefly, to return and then stop again, to do so yet another time or other times until ultimately the play reaches that point where the funniness of what was funny does not return, and the sources of the comic are mocked and denied.

I hope that the limited area with which this essay is concerned does not suggest that Pinter's plays are themselves so limited. They are not. And for all their compactness, they are large and rich. Yet his consistent employment of this particular tragicomic technique does suggest that this technique is one of the characteristics that define and distinguish his artistic signature.

The Room (1957, produced 1957)

Rose's extremely funny opening monologue reveals the sources of both the play's humor and the final denial of that humor. These sources are particularly noticeable in the first page and a half, which contains one-third of the monologue. The fact that Rose jabbers on, without as much as a peep from her husband Bert, is comic. In the final scene comes a reversal—Bert speaks, for the first time in the play, in what is practically a monologue—which ends laughter. When Riley begins to speak, Bert's eruption into violence prevents him from completing the sentence. As Rose talks

7. Of the Pinter canon, the following are not tragicomedies: the revue sketches, *A Night Out*, *Night School*, *The Dwarfs*, *Landscape*, *Silence*, and *Night*. The remaining plays, which constitute the bulk of his writing, I will examine in chronological sequence. For each play, I cite the year it was completed, then the year of its first production. When the year of completion is not known, only the year of first production is given. See Bibliographical Note for editions used and for comment on Pinter's revisions.

and talks in the first scene, often asking direct questions, she prepares and serves food to her husband, who utters no sound: a comic suggestion that he is very much the master of the house. At the end, the master asserts his authority by killing the intruder. At the opening of her monologue, Rose —revealing her aversion to the basement—compares it to her warm room, which is cosier and less damp. By the end of the play, a man from the dreaded basement has invaded her room. Verbs of sight pepper her monologue; for instance, "I looked out of the window," "I've never seen who it is." At the end of the play, she goes blind. During the first third of her monologue, Pinter provides one image of killing, a description of the coldness outside: "It's murder." At the end, Riley is murdered. The concluding scene, which denies the play's exclusively comic nature, revolves in part around possession (Bert's portion of the road), infringement of the room's security (Riley's presence), and speech (Bert's assertive speech, then Riley's attempted speech, which triggers Bert's violence).

The remaining two-thirds of the monologue repeats themes of the first third and continues images of sight ("It gets dark now") and death ("Those walls would have finished you off"). As the play progresses, images of blindness recur ("I could swear blind I've seen that before"), and Mrs. Sands repeats Rose's killing image: "It's murder out." Between opening monologue and closing catastrophe, comedy develops from themes that in the final scene are noncomic. The arrival of a visitor from outside is comic:

ROSE: . . . .
    A knock at the door. She stands.
    Who is it?
    Pause.
    Hallo!
    Knock repeated.
    Come in then.

Knock repeated.
Who is it?
Pause. The door opens and MR. KIDD *comes in.*
MR. KIDD: I knocked.

Laughter gradually diminishes with each successive intrusion. Laughter accompanies Kidd's initial appearance; a slight shock turns comic when the Sandses appear; with Kidd's second entry comes a premonition of danger; the visit of the man from the basement brings fear; when Bert returns, fear intensifies and laughter disappears. The source of part of the play's comedy is a hidden or forgotten past, connected with family, as Kidd's recollection that his sister may have resembled his mother, who may have been Jewish. "Yes, I wouldn't be surprised to learn that she was a Jewess. She didn't have many babies." Parents inform the comedy of Clarissa Sands's explanation, when Rose compliments her name. "My father and mother gave it to me." In the final scene, Riley's references to the past and Rose's father are no longer funny. A quest for someone is comic when the Sandses seek the landlord:

ROSE: Mr. Kidd. That's his name.
MR. SANDS: Well, that's not the bloke we're looking for.
ROSE: Well, you must be looking for someone else.

At the play's end, when Riley seeks Rose, or Sal, his quest is not comic. Sight connects to comedy, when Mr. Sands *"perches on the table"* and his wife claims he sat. "I saw you sit down," she insists, and he denies it: "You did not see me sit down because I did not sit bloody well down. I perched!" At the end, Rose's loss of sight is far from funny.

Notes of tension increase when the Sandses tell the apprehensive Rose about the man in the basement. At the conclusion of the tale, Rose catches Mrs. Sands in a contradiction: she just said they were coming downstairs when

Rose opened her door, whereas previously she had said they were going up. The Sandses' contradiction is an understandable error, but laughter at the comedy that derives from repetitions of the phrases "going up" and "coming down" begins to turn hollow when one recognizes the insecurity and fear that underlie the persistence of Rose's interrogation and the suspicion beneath her affable chitchat. The hollowness increases when Mr. Sands contradicts Rose's assertion that the house has no vacant rooms, for Number Seven, the man in the basement told him, is vacant. When Rose responds, "That's this room," then matters become no longer funny. As the Sandses leave, Rose does not say "goodbye," that is, "God be with you," but rather, "This room is occupied," a defiant assertion of possession. Nor does laughter return when old Mr. Kidd reenters. Only in Rose's double take when the blind Negro—whose entry is preceded by a proliferation of sight images—informs her his name is Riley, does comedy recur, but briefly. No longer jabbering away comically, Rose immediately pours out her hostility in a torrent of verbal abuse, and when Riley calls her Sal, she is terrified.

By the time Bert returns, laughter has ended and what had previously been comic is no longer so. What Bert sees upon his entrance is what might be construed as an intimate scene between his wife and the blind Negro: "*She touches his eyes, the back of his head and his temples with her hands. Enter* BERT." He stops, closes the curtains, looks at Rose carefully, and speaks. His words are powerful partly because they are his first in the play, and also because their suggestion of sex and violence ("I drove her down, hard," "I caned her," "I bumped him," "I had all my way") represents a veiled threat to the intruder and perhaps rival, as if Bert were daring Riley to take a false step. Only when Riley has the temerity to speak—"Mr. Hudd, your wife"—does Bert attack him, first verbally and then physically, even kicking his head several times against the gas stove until Riley is inert. In *his* home, Bert's behavior suggests, no one speaks without his leave. Rose then clutches her eyes and announces that she cannot see.

The domestic comedy that begins the play, based chiefly on a wife waiting on her husband and on the question of security, ends with the reassertion of the husband's supremacy, the destruction of an intruder into their haven, and the reinstatement of the status quo—which is the traditional ending of such comedy, where a threatened disruption from the outside fails to harm. But while the status quo is restored, harm occurs. The comedy is negated by fear, violence, death, and the debilitation of the mainstay of security. The home is no longer inviolable and the wife is now blind. Although the intruder is destroyed, the ending mocks happiness: the home is likewise destroyed.

The Birthday Party (1957, produced 1958)

Within its first three pages, *The Birthday Party* draws comedy from subjects that at the end of the play are no longer funny. The opening dialogue focuses upon identity:

MEG: Is that you, Petey?
Pause.
Petey, is that you?
Pause.
Petey?
PETEY: What?
MEG: Is that you?
PETEY: Yes, it's me.
MEG: What?

At the end of act 3, the question of an identity for Stanley, whom Goldberg proposes to make a new man, is no longer comic but ghastly. The next subject of comedy in act 1 is breakfast, the "nice" cornflakes Meg provides Petey and the "succulent" fried bread she serves Stanley. In act 3, by contrast, Meg has run out of cornflakes and Goldberg and McCann have had the last of the fried bread. She has no more breakfast left for Stanley, whose nourishment has been taken by the predators. The question of Stanley's whereabouts is comic at the start of act 1: "Is Stanley up yet?" "I don't know. Is he?" "I don't know. I haven't seen him down yet." "Well then, he can't be up." In act 3, however, the same initial question is no longer comic. In the newspaper story that Petey reads, birth is a source of comedy, and when Petey tells Meg that a girl has been born, Meg twice declares she would rather have a boy. Later she gives a little boy's drum to Stanley, who in act 2 has a birthday party, and in the final act, in ironic fulfillment of Meg's wish, Goldberg and McCann promise to make a new man of Stanley who is, in effect, reborn. Departure is also a source of humor in the early part of the play as Meg and Petey discuss Stanley taking her for a walk. At the end of the play, she and Stanley depart separately, and his departure is far from comic. Binding all five subjects of comedy is the comic technique of verbal repetition. At the end of act 3, Stanley's inability to speak is not at all funny. Not only does the humor of the play's first three pages revolve around identity, food, Stanley's whereabouts upstairs, birth, and departure, subjects that in act 3 provide no more laughter, it sets up a domestic comedy based on character and language. As the play progresses, the same subjects and technique turn to menace and become less exclusively comic, then not comic.

Although *The Birthday Party* does not employ the theatrical device of the play within a play, it contains analogues of this device—the reading of the newspaper story, songs and a recitation, and a party game—which, like the play within a play, employ one or more characters as audience and relate to the play's themes. As indicated, the newspaper story concerns birth, and a character-spectator comments with thematic appropriateness upon the story. In the second act, McCann performs, though he does not act: he sings two songs, between which he recites a line of another. The subject of his first song—"Glorio, Glorio, to the bold Fenian men!"—is strong Irishmen who will reclaim what is theirs, which suggests McCann's reclamation of Stanley. "The night that poor Paddy was stretched," McCann recites, "the boys they all paid him a visit." Although Stanley is destroyed by means other than hanging, "the boys," like those in the recitation, pay him a visit. Finally, McCann sings an entire stanza, which though sentimentally happy, fearfully resonates the play's thematic tones. While some say the Garden of Eden has vanished, sings McCann, he knows its location and gives directions to get there—a suggestion that he and Goldberg have found Stanley's hideaway. In the final two lines, McCann twice calls Paddy Reilly to return home with him—a link with the hanged Paddy of the recited line and with Stanley, whom he and Goldberg call to leave with them. Another analogy to the play within a play is playing; at the party, the characters participate in a game of blindman's buff.[8] As in the frame play, identity is a key factor in this party game, in which a blindfolded player attempts to catch and identify another player. The game turns deadly when Stanley becomes the blindman, and to accommodate the blindfold, Stanley must remove his glasses, which McCann breaks, thus blinding Stanley in the frame play as well as in the party game. As blindfolded Stanley is buffeted about, unaware of the other players' activities, so the Stanley of the frame play is buffeted about by Goldberg and McCann, whose actions he is unable to cope with effectively. As blindfolded Stanley attempts to strangle Meg, Stanley at the end of the frame play utters gurgling, incoherent sounds that suggest stran-

8. See also Michael W. Kaufman, "Actions that a Man Might Play: Pinter's *The Birthday Party*," *Modern Drama* 16 (September 1973): 167–78.

gulation. As the frame play begins comically and turns menacing, the game begins as amusement and turns to menace.

To return to act 1, Stanley's entry, unshaven and unkempt, reveals a comic but very human figure. In the third act, however, his attire no longer prompts laughter. His immaculate dress[9] reveals a defeated and deindividualized man, and neatness in this case inspires revulsion. One laughs when Stanley in act 1 finds the cornflakes horrible and the milk sour, pushes away his plate of fried bread, and calls the tea undrinkable muck. But the comedy of his lack of nourishment or sustenance erodes when he is unable to sustain himself in the face of danger. Early in the play, Stanley employs language effectively, and his use of the word *succulent* prompts laughter, whereas near the end of the play, Stanley's inability to utter an intelligible word evokes horror rather than laughter. In the first act, humor derives from Stanley's concern with his identity, when after going into a small tantrum about his tea he asks, "Tell me, Mrs. Boles, when you address yourself to me, do you ever ask yourself who exactly you are talking to? Eh?" Identity here is comic, for it is partly non sequitur, partly a foolish assertion of pride apparently out of proportion to the circumstances that provoke it. As the play develops, Stanley's sense of identity and of self erodes, as does the comedy associated with them.[10]

9. In the earlier edition, Stanley wears striped trousers, black jacket, and bowler hat; in the revised edition, he wears a dark, well-tailored suit that in the Royal Shakespeare Company's 1964 production, directed by Pinter, was identical to the suits of Goldberg and McCann.

10. In the earlier edition, but not the revised edition, Pinter in act 1 also links Goldberg and McCann to the subject of identity. Goldberg refers to his son, named "Emanuel. A quiet fellow. He never said much. Timmy I used to call him." "Emanuel?" asks Mc-

Foreshadowing such erosion are his references to his career as pianist, which in three successive sentences dwindle comically yet pathetically from "all over the world" to "all over the country" to "I once gave a concert." What is important is not whether Stanley performed several times, once, or at all but rather that Stanley makes these statements in this sequence, for verbally he nonentitizes himself, a development that anticipates the thrust of the play. Even Meg's supposed reinforcement of his professional status undercuts itself, since after twice asserting that she used to enjoy watching him play the piano and once affirming that he had been a pianist, she repeats his story about the concert and gets the facts wrong.

Frequently, aspects of act 1 provide laughter, but the same aspects fail to do so in act 3. In its childlike silliness and fantasy, Stanley's tale of people who will arrive in a van in search of someone is comic, and it terrifies Meg, whose fear is also comic. Yet when Goldberg and McCann remove Stanley in their car, the effect is not comic. Because of Stanley's obvious ineffectuality, his invitation to Lulu to go somewhere with him is funny: "But where could we go?" she asks, to which he replies, "Nowhere. There's nowhere to go. So we could just go. It wouldn't matter." Later in the play, when it becomes evident that Stanley cannot escape Goldberg and McCann, no matter where else he might flee, the words retrospectively turn unfunny. Even Goldberg and McCann themselves begin as comic figures: the comic

Cann. "That's right. Manny." "Manny?" "Sure. It's short for Emanuel." "I thought you called him Timmy." "I did." Apart from the fact that Timmy is unexpected because it is unrelated to the name Emanuel, the dialogue is comic in its rhythms and repetitions. Yet because the three names of Goldberg's son, each a mark of identification, result in a confusion about identity and ultimately a lack of identification, the humor anticipates the unfunny destruction of Stanley's identity.

Jew who spouts bourgeois platitudes and the comic Irishman who drinks whisky and sings. Some of their stichomythic dialogue resembles vaudeville patter: "Is this it?" "This is it." "Are you sure?" "Sure I'm sure." But undercutting the comic nature of the patter is a sense of mystery: "I didn't see a number on the gate," says McCann, and Goldberg comments, "I wasn't looking for a number." A source of laughter that becomes a source of fear is Meg's birthday gift, a boy's drum, funny since it is given to an adult, and funnier when Meg explains, "It's because you haven't got a piano." Yet the fun stops when Stanley beats the drum in an erratic, uncontrolled manner until, standing over her, his face and the drumbeat become *savage and possessed*." At this point, the climax of the first act—when Stanley loses control of himself, acts savagely, and behaves like a man possessed—laughter stops. The funny relationship between motherly Meg and her young lodger ceases to be funny. What shocks and horrifies in this climactic scene, moreover, points toward the play's resolution, also shocking and horrifying: physical threat, fear, Stanley's inability to coordinate his physical activities, and his helplessness in controlling his actions. But the conclusion of the first act does not conclude the play's comedy. Rather, the movement of the first act encapsulates the movement of the play as a whole.

Surprisingly, for after so brutal a curtain scene one would not anticipate mirth, comedy returns at the outset of act 2, where McCann tears a sheet of newspaper into five strips of equal width. Though comic because of the contrast between his serious attitude and the pointlessness of the activity, the strips of newspaper prompt no laughter when Stanley picks one up. Immediately, McCann *"moves in"*: "Mind that. . . . Leave it." Comic and noncomic coexist when Goldberg, in a tribute to birthdays, transforms an ode to birth into a paean about "a corpse waiting to be washed" and announces that such a viewpoint cheers him. Comic, the speech also anticipates the fate of Stanley, whose birthday becomes a rebirth that will leave him like a thoroughly scrubbed corpse. It is during Stanley's interrogation by Goldberg and McCann, however, that comedy diminishes, then ceases. With Stanley accused of having killed his wife and never having married, of treason and nosepicking, the humor derives from non sequitur and contradiction, which become decreasingly funny as the persistent rhythm of threat and menace increases. When both interrogators tell Stanley he is dead, laughter stops once more. Condemned, Stanley resembles, in the phrase that was initially funny, "a corpse waiting to be washed." When the party begins, comedy returns; but the party ends in terror as Stanley giggles eerily over Lulu's spreadeagled body. Like the first act, the second encapsulates the movement of the play as a whole; but in act 2, the play's rhythm accelerates, for laughter stops and returns, then does so again, stopping for longer periods each time.

Lulu is the focus of a subplot that provides most of the few laughs of act 3, where comedy has diminished and fear increased. The story of which she is pivot parallels that of Stanley, for Goldberg invades her sanctuary and "ruins" her, and in the third act he and McCann interrogate her as savagely but more comically than they had interrogated Stanley in act 2. Unlike Stanley, however, Lulu successfully escapes, a getaway that tends partly to mitigate the horror associated with Stanley's fate.

Act 3 repeats, in a manner no longer funny, subjects and patterns of act 1. Its opening recalls that of act 1, for it employs similar locutions between the same principals:

MEG: Is that you, Stan? (*Pause.*) Stanny?
PETEY: Yes.

MEG: Is that you?
PETEY: It's me.
MEG: *(appearing at the hatch)*:   Oh, it's you.

The point of similarity with act 1 makes its difference from act 1 more striking, for in the first act Meg accurately identifies the man but in the third act she mistakes his identity—an ominous hint, perhaps, concerning the identity of the man she thinks has entered. In a gambit about whether Stanley is up or down, similar to that of the first act, Meg's and Petey's exchange is no longer comic, for Petey fails to respond with the repeated phrases and rhythms he had employed in act 1. Whereas act 1 derives humor from Meg's announcement that she is going upstairs to wake Stanley and from her actually doing so, Petey in act 3 orders her not to do so, and no laughter results. It is when Stanley enters, however, that laughter stops suddenly and with finality. The Stanley of the third act is not the unkempt comic figure of the first act but a cleanly dressed man who can neither see nor utter articulate sounds—a washed and walking corpse, as it were, or in McCann's phrase, "a dead duck." A supposedly happy ending—a new, prosperous, and socially approved life for a young man—Stanley's fate denies the joy associated with a new life, denies life itself. Meg's affirmation of a happy time, appropriate to the conclusion of a comedy, negates itself by its overinsistence and inaccuracy, which erode the joy: "I was the belle of the ball. . . . They all said I was. . . . Oh, it's true. I was. . . . I know I was." Also destructive of the happiness usually associated with such a speech is the spectator's knowledge that Meg has yet to discover that Stanley has departed.

The conclusion of this tragicomedy contains no happiness, and what had been sources of laughter at the play's start—identity, nourishment, the whereabouts of Stanley, birth, and departure—are no longer sources of laughter at its end. With each new act, the amount of comedy has decreased and the amount of terror increased. Comedy and its cessation function organically in *The Birthday Party*, where the renewal of laughter, a release for the audience, suggests a reprieve for Stanley, and its cessation suggests his entrapment, which at the end of the play is conclusive.

The Dumb Waiter (1957, produced 1959)

In the opening pantomime of *The Dumb Waiter*, Ben reads a paper while Gus ties his shoelaces with difficulty, walks slowly toward the inside door, stops, unties a lace, removes a shoe to discover a flattened matchbox, and then removes his other shoe to find an empty cigarette packet, also flattened. Although one hesitates to overload a short comic scene with heavy symbolism, the pantomime comically hints at a noncomic conclusion, for the absence of cigarettes and matches symbolizes the depletion of Gus's sustenance, and their condition anticipates his dishevelment and danger of imminent destruction.

In subject and symbol, the opening three-page dialogue contains sources of comedy that at the end of the play prompt no laughter. The major concern of this dialogue, two newspaper stories, function, like the newspaper story in *The Birthday Party*, as analogies to the play within a play. In the first story, an octogenarian who tries to cross a busy, traffic-laden street by crawling under a stationary truck is killed when the truck starts and runs over him. Hilarious, partly because the situation is so preposterous and partly because of the seriousness of Ben's and Gus's superior-sounding comments upon the old man's foolishness (and not upon the fact of his death), the episode anticipates the tableau of imminent death that concludes the play and, before that tableau, the similar, abbreviated, and no longer superior remarks about the same story, which this time is not read aloud. At the start of the play, death elsewhere is comic; at its conclusion, imminent death is no longer comic. In the second newspaper story, the death is murder: an eight-year-old girl who killed a cat while her brother looked on. Part of the humor of this story derives from the fact that the paper carries so inconsequential a news item, part from verbal niceties ("How did he do it?" "It was a girl." "How did she do it?"), but the largest part derives from the men's transformation of the story into a silly whodunit with a far-fetched ending: the men agree her brother did it and blamed it on her. More suggestively than the first, the second newspaper story comically foreshadows the final relationship of the two men, for it deals not with accidental death but with murder (no matter which child did it) and as the men interpret the story, one person is the victim of the other. At the end of the play, which is not comic, one of the men may be murdered, a victim of the other.

Between beginning and end, laughter results from speech and situations that recur after laughter stops. With comic derision, Ben tells the complaining Gus, "You kill me"—ironically, it turns out, for at the conclusion of the play it is Ben who may kill Gus. Although Gus's various complaints—about the amount of time it takes the capricious toilet to fill, his inability to sleep restfully, the lack of sufficient blankets, his being stuck indoors so often, the organization's inadequate concern for their comfort—are funny, they also point to a malaise that may result in the dissatisfied killer becoming a victim at the hands of his partner, who finds working conditions satisfactory. They survive who only wait dumbly, the play may suggest—its title refers to a dumb waiter, whereas the object on the upstage wall is a one-word dumbwaiter—and Gus no longer waits dumbly. He thinks, and he questions various aspects of his job. Although most of his questions are funny, the fact that he asks them portends something fearful, as Ben's nervous response may intimate: "You're always asking me questions. . . . Stop wondering. You've got a job to do. Why don't you just do it and shut up?" Yet the play does not at this point become tense, for Gus, responding to the "job" reference and not to shutting up, raises questions about the job. Though comedy persists, it is undercut when the gunmen's superiors take the side of the unquestioning killer. While Gus appears to win a victory over the dispute as to whether "light the kettle" or "put on the kettle" is the correct expression, for Ben, who had insisted on the former, unthinkingly employs the latter, Gus's victory is temporary. Later in the play, Ben triumphantly reports that the voice from the speaking tube uses the expression "light the kettle." Although this side-taking is comic, Ben's superior position at the close of the play denies comedy, for he points a gun at a defenseless Gus.

The activities of the dumbwaiter, which clangs down without warning, gives orders, then clangs up again without warning, while the two gunmen scurry to obey its commands, are very funny indeed. But what the audience sees is two men who serve an unseen commander from above. No matter that he is human, Gus and Ben are visually in the position of mortals who obey an invisible, omnipotent deity, and it is this stage image that registers. Within its framework, Gus appears frantic, irresolute, unable to cope, and Ben calmer, more resolute, self-possessed. Whereas Gus questions what to do and pleads for more time to think, Ben makes decisions about what to do, even tells Gus that certain things, such as shouting, are not done. Whereas Gus had secretly hoarded sustenance, Ben orders him to divest himself of it and send it up the dumbwaiter. Although the situation is comic, the depletion of Gus's resources anticipates the loss of his capabilities and the increasing stature of Ben anticipates his commanding position. The disparity between the demands for unusual food and Gus's inadequate substitutes provides a source of comedy, but the sight of

Gus emptying all he has in order to satisfy an unseen master, which he fails to do, undercuts the humor. Without matches, without the means to light the stove when he obtains matches, emptying his insides during his frequent trips to the lavatory, the play suggests that Gus, unlike Ben, has nothing upon which he can rely. "I could do with a bit of sustenance," says Gus, suggesting more than he intends. The comedy of the godlike dumbwaiter's rejection of Gus's offerings turns noncomic when at the play's curtain Gus himself is rejected.

Following the episode of the dumbwaiter comes the point where laughter stops. As Ben and Gus review their instructions, Gus's repetitions of Ben's statements are hilarious, as is Gus's recognition that Ben has omitted the instruction concerning Gus's possession of a gun. But then laughter stops. Apparently accidental, the omission is significant in that it foreshadows the play's end, when Gus has no gun. Perhaps Gus recognizes the implications of what has occurred in the room, for he is *"deep in thought"* and *"troubled."* More intensely than before, he questions Ben, but his questions are no longer funny. When the dumbwaiter sends the next order, Gus shrieks maniacally into the speaking tube that they have nothing left, though the plural pronoun he employs may stand more readily for himself alone and the reference may be to more than food. Now there is no more comic scurrying about. With nothing left, Gus is at the end of his resources. At this point, the two men repeat their responses to the newspaper stories, now read silently, and now unfunny, perhaps because the subject of death, no longer spoken aloud, is a present fear. When Gus departs for the lavatory, the speaking tube gives Ben instructions. Although Ben's response suggests that as far as he is concerned the instructions are for both ("Sure we're ready," he says twice), the actual command may have been ambiguous, for "you" is singular as well as plural. Preparing to do his job, Ben calls for Gus to enter, which he does, but from the door of the victim, as a victim, stripped of his jacket, holster, and revolver, and stooped, facing Ben's gun. With this tableau the play ends. Comic at the opening of the play, death is not comic at its close. Comic tales of victims start the play, a noncomic vision of Gus as victim concludes it. An amusing apparent error in the repetition of instructions is at the end of the play no longer amusing when the same situation is actualized. The comic deprivation of Gus's resources turns unfunny when Gus may be deprived of his life.

The simplicity of the tragicomic structure of *The Dumb Waiter* endows the play with an apparent purity of tone that is both appropriate and deceptive, indeed appropriate because it is deceptive. The dialogue, preoccupations, and activities of the two men are comically absurd. Directly, the comic play proceeds to a point where comedy stops and death becomes imminent: a straightforward movement to a place where a reversal occurs. But the purity of tone is only apparent. The comic dialogue, preoccupations, and activities are those of two hired killers, a profession not normally associated with laughter. Even when one of them takes out a gun for the first time, the action is funny, for it seems in context an exaggerated response to an envelope of matches that someone has slipped under the door. Aptly, what appears purely comic deceives, for death and divestiture of resources (perhaps including life itself) underlie that comedy and finally deny it.

A Slight Ache (1958, produced 1959)

At the start, *A Slight Ache* suggests a comedy based on marital bickering, with its misunderstandings, mutual irritation, and correction of errors. At the end, the marriage dissolves as husband and other man exchange places. At the play's start, wife and husband breakfast; at its end, she invites the husband's replacement to lunch. In the first scene, Edward and Flora discuss the various flowers that grow in their garden. At the end of the play, she invites the Matchseller to see the same flowers in what is at that time "my garden, your garden." Whereas observation of flora at the start of the play provides humor, references to flowers at the play's end are no longer funny. "You know perfectly well what grows in your garden," Flora tells Edward at the conclusion of the opening segment of dialogue, but he corrects her, "It is clear that I don't." Imperceptive about flora and Flora at the start, he cannot visually perceive either at the end, and what is funny about his imperception at the start of the play is no longer funny at its conclusion. Sight, a prominent concern of the play, is frequently a verbal concern as well. "Have you noticed the honeysuckle?" asks Flora in the play's opening line, and Edward responds, "I must look." In the final part of his last speech, he employs the verb "to see" in its past tense.

Following an expository opening about flowers is the episode of the wasp, an intruder who is a source of laughter for us and fear for the characters; this wasp is the first of two intruders and a foreshadowing of a later malady. Edward's and Flora's bickering about whether insects bite, sting, or suck is funny. Also comic is the actual destruction of the wasp, as Edward pours hot water through the spoon hole of a pot, "blinding him," as Edward declares, and destroying him. As the wasp is comically destroyed in the marmalade by scalding water, Edward is later destroyed, not comically, in the presence of the Matchseller, whose body he says is like jelly.

When Edward in the dark scullery peers at the Matchseller, who stands in the blazing sun, the stage image suggests the viewpoint of the wasp who peered out of the spoonhole. "What a farce," Edward exclaims as he comments on the Matchseller, a generic observation that later changes at the precise point where laughter stops. Intending "to get to the bottom of" the question of the Matchseller's presence and to "get rid of him" from the gate, the disproportion between Edward's determination and the mere fact of an old man standing outside with a matchtray provokes laughter. When Edward later gets what he says he wants, the ironic result no longer causes laughter, for Edward and the Matchseller exchange places.

Edward's first interview with the Matchseller arouses laughter, partly from the verbal repetitions—such as, "I say, can you hear me? *(Pause.)* I said, I say, can you hear me?"—partly because of the sexually suggestive names of the liquor Edward offers his guest—such as "Focking Orange" and "Fuchsmantel Reisling"—and partly because of Edward's sheer ineffectuality in prompting a response. Yet these same sources later deny comedy when speech reveals itself as a mask for insecurity, when Flora switches her sexual allegiance, and when ineffectuality turns to psychological deterioration. At the end of this scene, moreover, in a sudden verbal shift from comic ("Chair comfortable? I bought it in a sale. I bought all the furniture in this house in a sale. The same sale.") to noncomic ("When I was a young man. You too, perhaps. You too, perhaps. . . . At the same time, perhaps!"), Edward moves from the subject of his sole possession to a link with the Matchseller. Ending the scene, his statement about their possible connection anticipates the noncomic end of the play.

Yet the cessation of laughter is temporary, for away from the strange Matchseller, Edward regains his absurd poise and describes the silent guest as "reticent" and "not a drinking man." Sandwiched between Edward's two interviews with the Matchseller is Flora's, in which laughter tenuously highlights noncomic sexuality (after describing her rape, Flora begins to seduce the Matchseller), noncomic chiefly because it involves a betrayal of Edward but also because she connects sexuality with a man's childlike dependence, which she then links to death. Within half a dozen lines she erotically whispers to the Matchseller, "till death do us part. . . . I'm going to put you to bed and watch over you. . . . And I'll buy you . . . little toys to play with. On your deathbed. Why shouldn't you die happy?"

Edward's second interrogation forcefully recalls the wasp in the marmalade jar: he closes the blinds and curtains, then comments on the darkness. Although the scene contains the same type of verbal comedy as the earlier scenes ("The house . . . was polished, all the banisters were polished, and the stair rods, and the curtain rods. . . . My desk was polished, and my cabinet. . . . I was polished."), as well as comedy based on recollection of the good old days (which include the same day, when Edward heroically poured hot water down the spoon hole), the comedy of Edward's disintegrating verbal dexterity ("You looked quite different without a head—I mean without a hat") suggests his psychological deterioration. When he crumbles to the tragicomic point where laughter stops, Pinter signals this moment: Edward changes his reference from laughter to tears. "Ah, that's good for a guffaw, is it?" he asks the Matchseller. "That's good for a belly laugh." But then *He catches his breath* and recognizes, "You haven't been laughing. You're crying." Whether the Matchseller laughs at or grieves for him, or neither, comedy ends. The ache in Edward's eyes increases, his sight worsens, he falls to the floor, and the Matchseller rises. Whereas early in the play Edward's desire to learn the Matchseller's identity is funny, his last, whispered words, "Who are you?" represent a *"final effort"* that is not funny. Summer arrives, food is ready, flowers bloom, but while all of these manifestations usually carry associations of comedy, these same manifestations at the end of *A Slight Ache*, in the presence of an utterly defeated

Edward, mock and deny comedy. Unlike *The Dumb Waiter*, which proceeds inexorably to a surprising reversal that denies the comedy that precedes it, *A Slight Ache* proceeds just as inexorably to a reversal that does not surprise, for in depicting Edward's increasingly annoying eyeache, his psychological deterioration, his wife's infidelity, and above all the moments where laughter temporarily stops within individual scenes, the playwright prepares his audience for the devastating denial at the play's conclusion of its initially comic nature.

The Caretaker (produced 1960)

In a silent, prologue-like scene that opens the play, Mick, alone, slowly surveying a room filled with junk, observes each object in it, then sits still. Upon hearing the muffled voices of his brother and Davies, he quickly departs. Anticipatory, the scene is neither comic nor noncomic. It establishes a man in a room. Since no one else is present and since he betrays no nervousness, he may belong there. But because he wears a jacket and faces front while apparently waiting, he may be a visitor. When he unobtrusively leaves upon hearing voices, his swift departure indicates he may be an intruder. Such inferences anticipate essential questions of the play. Who belongs in the room? Who is the intruder? Moreover, this pantomime, which precedes the first spoken scene of the play, is echoed by a briefer pantomime that precedes the final scene of the play, which itself echoes the first spoken scene. In the later pantomime, the same character looks not at objects but at his brother, who looks at him. *"Both are smiling, faintly."* Although Mick begins to speak, he does not get far.[11] As before, he leaves. Whereas the earlier pantomime establishes tension, the later

11. In the earlier edition, Mick says nothing. In the revised edition, he utters only a word ("Look") and grunts.

reveals friendly communication between brothers, an essentially comic note. Both pantomimes contrast with the dialogue that follows.

Within the first few pages of dialogue, *The Caretaker* establishes avenues that are either comic (productive of laughter) or associated with comedy (friendliness). The play's final scene denies the exclusiveness of both avenues. Whereas the play begins with Aston bringing Davies into the room, it ends with his refusal to permit him to stay. The play's first words are, "Sit down." At the end, Aston asks Davies to leave. In the first few pages, Davies talks of his having been rejected by others, a contrast to Aston's acceptance of him. At the end, he talks of Aston's having accepted him earlier, in contrast to his present rejection of him. At the start, Aston offers Davies tobacco, which he takes for his pipe. At the end, Davies returns "for my pipe," but Aston offers him nothing.[12] Whereas in the first spoken scene Aston offers to help Davies, in the last scene Davies offers to help Aston, who refuses his assistance. At the play's start, as Aston fiddles with the plug of an electric toaster in an effort to fix it, Davies talks of himself and says nothing of his host's activities. In the final scene, Aston fiddles with what Davies pointedly calls "the same plug," but this time Davies encourages him and Aston ignores the old man's statements. Whereas Aston first listens to Davies, who ignores him much of the time, Aston largely ignores Davies in the final scene. In the early part of the play, all of Davies's stories, which are comic, concern his rejection or eviction: his employer fired him, a monk told him to leave, and despite his assertion that he rejected his wife it was he rather than she who left their home. At the end, when the brothers reject and evict him, their actions, which are not comic, deny the exclusiveness of the comedy that is based on rejection and evic-

12. In the earlier version, Aston asks Davies whether he found the pipe. In the revised version, he says nothing at all on the subject.

tion. Much of the humor of the early part of the play derives from a grubby, crotchety old man's excessive preoccupation with himself, his mumblings and complaints, his real or feigned self-esteem, his unresponsiveness to one who treats him kindly, and the contrast between what he says ("I've had dinner with the best") and how he looks (virtually the worst). By the end of the play, comedy no longer derives from these same characteristics, and far from insisting he is clean, Davies begs for confirmation that he is ("You didn't mean that, did you, about me stinking, did you?"), but he does not receive it. At first, an old wreck's assertions of dignity prompt laughter, but finally, laughter leaves in the face of a pathetic, dirty old man who has lost what little he had. The essential characteristics of the old man remain, but not the comedy once associated with them.

Laughter results when Davies grumbles that the shoes Aston gives him do not fit, and as his feet fail to fit his benefactor's shoes, so he fails to fit into his benefactor's flat. The early part of the play reveals comically that neither the name Davies uses nor the bag of possessions he carries are his; the later part reveals noncomically that the flat is not to be his either. In the first act, humor derives from Davies's inept efforts to ingratiate himself with Aston, but the final scene, in which he similarly tries to ingratiate himself, denies that humor. In the first act, Davies's refusal to answer Aston's questions about where he comes from is comic (he hedges even about where he was born), whereas at the end, Aston's refusal to respond to Davies's question, "Where am I to go?" denies humor. Whereas the first act is essentially comic, its shocking ending—wherein Mick brutally intimidates Davies—stops the comedy and encapsulates the thrust of the play: comically, Davies, who considers himself in possession of the flat, examines it as if it belonged to him, whereupon its owner, ending the comedy, makes clear that it does not.

Laughter returns shortly after the start of the second act when Mick, after having victimized the old man, asks whether he slept well. What Mick does, however, is to destroy insidiously though comically the old man's equilibrium and undermine his very identity. Mick associates Davies with such a flood of place names as to deny his association with any place, a comic anticipation of the noncomic denial of Davies's association with the flat. Comedy and threat merge in Mick's superficially friendly identification of Davies, which results in destruction not only of Davies's identity but also of his sex, for after imprecisely declaring that Davies reminds him of his "uncle's brother" (does the phrase mean Mick's father or another brother of his father?), he denies the resemblance when he tells the decrepit old Caucasian that the relative who was built like him was a "bit of an athlete" and was perhaps part American Indian. Mick finally destroys Davies's sexual identity when he asserts that this man, Davies's "spitting image," one day "married a Chinaman." Comically, Davies is cancelled, nonentitized, and nullified as later he will be noncomically.

Despite the shock of its beginning, a carry-over from the end of act 1, most of act 2 provokes laughter. In a dramatic shift at the end of act 2, when Aston begins his long monologue about his hospital experiences, laughter stops. Whereas early in the play, Davies's description of his past was funny, Aston's description of his own past is not funny. For the first time, moreover, Aston is absorbed in himself and does not attend to the self-absorbed old man. This scene visually reveals the self-absorption of Aston and his exclusion of Davies: "*During* ASTON's *speech the room grows darker. By the close of the speech only* ASTON *can be seen clearly.* DAVIES *and all the other objects are in the shadow.*" Although comedy reemerges in the next act, Aston's speech points to his later, more conclusive rejection of Davies, when laughter finally ends.

Act 3 consists of a series of defeats for Davies. Each of the first four scenes that follow its opening pantomime is comic, then reaches a point where laughter stops. In the fifth and final scene, when Davies is utterly rejected, the exclusiveness of the play's comic elements is utterly denied. In the first scene, Mick describes in glowing and comically vivid detail his plans to decorate the flat. Abruptly, the comic description of the palatial transformation of the cluttered flat ends:

DAVIES: Who would live there?
MICK: I would. My brother and me.
   Pause.
DAVIES: What about me?

Mick does not respond, as later Aston fails to respond when Davies begs permission to stay. But Mick is not yet done tantalizing Davies. In the second scene, Aston gives a pair of shoes and shoelaces to Davies, who is dissatisfied, for the shoes do not fit and the laces do not match them. His rejection of Aston, still comic because of his crotchetiness, receives a noncomic edge when Aston rejects Davies: unnoticed by the old man, recalling the end of act 2 and anticipating the end of act 3, he quietly leaves the room. In the third scene, after Davies whines, complains, and reviles his benefactor, comedy stops, for he flashes a knife at Aston, who then tells him to leave. Arrogantly, the imperceptive Davies insists that Aston must leave, and he strikes at a subject about which Aston is sensitive, the shed, which he calls "stinking." But Davies rather than the shed stinks, says Aston, who ignores the knife and packs the ineffectual old man's belongings. With a threat, Davies departs. The fourth scene follows the same pattern. Davies, who had been offered a caretaker job first by Aston and then by Mick, was rejected by Aston and is now rejected by Mick, who verbally abuses him when he insults Mick's brother, and in a burst of violence Mick breaks the statue of the Buddha. The violence that concludes this penultimate stage in the rejection of Davies—a rejection that is underscored in the scene's final line, wherein Davies repeats what he had asked in the first scene of act 3, "What about me?"—is less conclusive, however, than the nonviolent, silent rejection of Davies by his erstwhile benefactor. Nevertheless, this violence conclusively ends the play's comedy; from this point until the end of the play, no laughter remains. To Davies's repeated pleas for reinstatement in the final scene, Aston either says no—a word he utters four times—or he remains silent. Visually, Davies's rejection is striking, for while spectators hear either *no* or silence in response to his pleas, they see a stage image of that rejection: Aston stands at the window, his back to the old man.

Each of the first two acts, and the first four scenes of the final act, employ the pattern of the play as a whole: "funny up to a point. Beyond that point it ceases to be funny," to repeat Pinter's accurate description. This pattern, moreover, which increases in tempo in the third act, reinforces an important thematic aspect of the play. At each point where laughter stops, its cessation signals a reversal from security to insecurity for Davies. At the end of act 1, laughter stops when Mick physically threatens him. At the end of act 2, it stops when Aston psychologically excludes him, though the comedy of the second act, unlike that of the first, has a noncomic edge, since the audience perceives Mick's threat to Davies, whom Mick deceives. In each of the first four scenes of act 3, laughter stops with the rejection or departure of the old man. In the fifth and final scene of act 3, laughter does not return, for Davies's rejection is complete.

But the pathetic old man is not a tragic figure. Rather, he is the bumbling author of his own folly, whose symbolic annihilation denies the exclusiveness of the comedy usually associated with such a person. While laughter has stopped, however, one avenue associated with comedy has not: friendliness. Instead, it has shifted. Whereas Aston's initial friendliness toward Davies has vanished by the end of the play, friendliness itself remains, for the two brothers have reunited. Whereas the man who wanted to be caretaker is denied that job, Aston and Mick accept it: Aston plans to take care of the shed by himself, and Mick, protecting his brother from intruders, takes care of him. Tragicomic, *The Caretaker* erodes the laughter that began its dialogue as, simultaneously, it affirms a family unit and denies an old fool dignity.

The Collection (produced 1961)

At the start, Pinter establishes a comedy based on two interlocking sexual triangles, a heterosexual couple and the woman's lover, and a homosexual couple and the wife of the other couple. Since the dramatic question is neither "Will she (or he) leave her (or his) partner for a new lover?" nor "Whodunit?" (the identity of the lover), but rather "Were the apparent lovers lovers in fact?" this last, Pirandellian question denies the purely comic and signals a turn toward tragicomedy. Certainty about the alleged commission of the deed gives the possible doers power over their uncertain partners.

In the first part of the play, sex, marriage, language, and a quest for truth provide sources of laughter, whereas in the final scene they do not. The first three scenes introduce all four characters. James's first words to Harry, on the telephone, constitute a search for verification that underlies the entire play: "Is that you, Bill?" When Harry replies that Bill is in bed, James asks what with only a change of tense is the dramatic question that underlies the play's action, "What's he doing in bed?" In the final part of the play, the question of what Bill did in bed, desperately raised, is no longer funny. Comedy is more subtle in the second scene. Preparing to leave for work, Stella exasperatedly asks James whether he will go to work that day or be at home that evening. Though his answer to the first question is negative, he gives no reply to the second. At the end of the play, their situation is uncomically reversed: it is he who persistently questions, she who does not reply. In the third scene, comedy derives from a phallic symbol, marital bickering, and jealousy. Elegantly attired in a dressing gown, Harry trips on a stair rod as he descends the stairs. After marital-like bickering about the stair rod and then about breakfast, Harry mentions James's phone call, which he connects with Bill's trip to the dress collection the previous week. "You must have met lots of people." "I didn't speak to a soul." "Must have been miserable for you." These sources inform the final section of the play, where laughter ceases. At the end of the scene, James's arrival, following Bill's departure, signals a desire for verification, and though this attempt is comic in scene 3 ("I think you've got the wrong man." "I think you have." "I don't think you know anything about it."), the effort is not comic at the play's end, where James is uncertain he has the right man or knows anything about "it," although the word then has a different referent.

The verbal sparring between Bill and James in their first scene is extremely funny, and even Bill's outrageous pun amuses (he plans to stand for Parliament, where he will become "minister for Home Affairs"), yet not only does their sparring turn unfunny when James threatens Bill with a knife at the end of the play, but even the end of the scene denies the exclusively comic. Perhaps accurately, perhaps mischievously, Bill comments on James's statement that in Leeds he was sitting on the bed beside James's wife: "Not sitting. Lying."

In the next scene, where Harry questions Bill about

his visitor, the dialogue, which centers on the effect of church bells, suggests the question of Bill's adultery with James's wife. Whereas Harry's hostility emerges as verbal comedy when he describes Bill's visitor, that hostility becomes vicious during the "slum slug" speech later in the play.

Near the end of the play, laughter ceases and what had seemed comic becomes tragicomic. Although the sexually suggestive dialogue between Bill and James amuses, for it provides a prospect of a homosexual triangle in addition to the other configurations, James's suddenly putting an end to words, "for fun," he claims, puts an end to fun, which it denies. He proposes "a mock duel," and its amusement is James's alone, for he duels seriously, and the mockery is his alone, directed at Bill. Laughter ends when James actually throws a knife at Bill, who deflects it with his hand, which becomes scarred. Viciously, James reminds his formerly cocksure host that earlier he had denied having a scar as a result of his encounter with Stella. Following James's actual knifing, Harry employs verbal knifing as he reminds Bill of Bill's slum origins and dependence upon himself. Wounded by Harry's verbal assault as he had been by James's physical assault, Bill strikes back with words, which wound Harry because they contradict what Harry had just heard. When James returns to his wife to obtain verification of Bill's story, her silence places him in a vulnerable position. In the *"half light"* that ends the play, Pinter reveals the two couples, each reflective of the other, each containing a man shattered or insecure because his mate's response has made him uncertain of sexual infidelity, and therefore insecure about his relationship with his partner, who may become, because of his or her certainty, more dominant than before.

What had begun as a possible comedy based on interlocking sexual triangles has become a tragicomedy based on uncertainty about those triangles. Although each couple reunites at the end of *The Collection*, their reunions do not constitute returns to the status quo, for the unknowing member of each couple has been psychologically shattered. At the start of the play, each believed he would receive a definitive answer to his question concerning his partner's infidelity. At its end, each is certain only that he will remain uncertain. Because of that uncertainty, he is insecure and can be dominated by his partner. Such psychological deterioration constitutes a denial of comedy. But since the couples neither divorce nor separate, their reunions harmonize with the conventional conclusion of domestic comedy. Pinter's tragicomic conclusion denies and mocks the exclusively comic basis of the play.

The Lover (produced 1963)

As with *The Collection*, sex is an important basis of *The Lover*, whose opening suggests a comedy of manners. Unlike the earlier play, however, the cuckolded husband is complaisant about the visits of his wife's lover, and it is his agreeable and matter-of-fact acquiescence that creates much of the comedy. Both stage directions and opening line set the tone of these early scenes. "*Amiably*," Richard asks, "Is your lover coming today?" Although his departure follows an apparently sincere wish that his wife will have a pleasant afternoon, the scene establishes three distinct personae in a comic situation that at the end of the play will deny the exclusiveness of such comedy as the distinctions between two of these personae disappear. The conventional ending such a setup suggests is either a victory of the husband over the intruder or a continuation of a comfortable status quo—both comic conclusions. The actual ending denies the exclusiveness of comedy.

Much of the humor of these early scenes derives from an inversion of the husband's conventional attitudes. Richard discusses the situation as casually as if his wife's visitor were a maiden aunt: "Pleasant afternoon?" "Oh yes. Quite marvelous." "Your lover came, did he?" "Mmnn. Oh yes." "Did you show him the hollyhocks?" This sort of comedy increases when they discuss his mistress. Based on situations so familiar to theatergoers, comedy results not only from the casual but also from the clinical discussions of such situations ("She's simply a whore," says the husband of his extramarital partner, "a functionary who either pleases or displeases") juxtaposed beside clichés ("Frankness at all costs. Essential to a healthy marriage. Don't you agree?").

While Pinter hints at erosion when the couple argues about who first needed to look outside marriage for satisfaction, the relationship between Richard and Sarah appears basically to be mutually satisfactory. When, at about midpoint, Sarah's lover arrives to reveal himself as the husband in different costume, the situation changes, for in the second part of the play, husband-lover and wife-whore play a variety of sexual games. Less funny than the discursive comedy that precedes them, though funny still, these sex scenes deny the exclusively comic nature of the previous discussion, for the reality that was the basis of the comic dialogue is far different from what the audience had been led to believe. By the end of the lover's visit his threat to end the situation further denies (but does not entirely destroy) the exclusively comic nature of what the play has established, for the threat is psychological (and therefore serious) rather than situational (common to a comedy of this type). Even when the husband too insists that his wife's affair end, the denial of the exclusiveness of the comedy does not deny comedy altogether, for Pinter extracts humor from the husband's inappropriately businesslike dialogue and action: "Perhaps you would give him my compliments, by letter if you like, and ask him to cease his visits from (*He consults calendar.*)—the twelfth inst."

It is when the separate worlds merge—the husband takes the bongo drum from the hall cupboard and employs it in a menacing yet sexual manner—that laughter stops. Even a second reference to lovers (several, this time) who come to see the wife's hollyhocks, funny at the play's start, is not funny the second time. In this final scene, roles merge. Verbal comedy about different personae or different roles is no longer possible. When Richard in the final scene tells Sarah, "You're trapped," he refers to the situation in the sexual game they perform, but his words resonate further, as does her agreement. While the husband-suit and wife-dress are present, husband and wife are gone. Lover and whore, triumphant, are in their places. Although the husband tries to banish the lover, the lover banishes the husband—hence the play's title, which is singular rather than plural. It refers not to a couple or to a situation, but to one person, who in a sexual triangle seems to emerge victorious over the husband.

A denial of the expectations aroused at the start of what appeared to be a comedy about sex, the conclusion of *The Lover*, though not sad, is a tragicomic denial of the exclusive attributes of such comedy. Does the lover defeat the husband? Not exactly: it is the husband who in the role of lover defeats himself. Does the husband defeat the lover? Not exactly: the husband wins not as husband but as lover. Like *The Collection*, *The Lover* ends with reunion rather than separation, but also like *The Collection*, the reunion has shattered the foundations of the status quo, and therefore it mocks the exclusiveness of that situation's comic aspects.

The Homecoming (produced 1965)

As in *The Lover*, an unanticipated sexual arrangement concludes the action of *The Homecoming*. Comic at the start, an erosive process increasingly undercuts the comedy until laughter stops, and the sources that had aroused laughter deny it.

The three-and-a-half-page opening scene between Max and Lenny anticipates the final scene, which begins when Ruth invites Teddy, just before he leaves, not to become a stranger. At the beginning of the play, in a womanless household, Max enters from the kitchen, looking for scissors—an area and an implement usually associated with women. At the end, a woman is installed in the household by the men, who expect her to fulfill womanly functions. At the beginning, Max addresses Lenny, who responds either with abuse or silence, both productive of laughter. At the end, Max addresses Ruth, whose silence produces no laughter. Initially, Max's admission that he is getting old amuses; at the close of the play, his desperate denial of old age does not. In the opening scene, his mixed expression of love and hatred toward his late wife is comic. In the closing scene, his similar ambivalence toward Ruth, whom he accuses of trickery and begs for a kiss, is not. At the start, Max asserts his instinctive understanding of female horses, whose reliability, he declares, he could tell by smelling them and looking them straight in their eyes. At the end, by the same means, which are no longer funny, he maintains that Ruth is unreliable: "I can smell it!" he exclaims, and "*He looks up at her. . . . He raises his face to her.*"

Yet the comedy of the play's opening scene is not unrelievedly funny, for savagery underlies it. "I'll chop your spine off, you talk to me like that!" Max tells his son. Violence permeates the play. Max is a former butcher, Joey a boxer, and Lenny a pimp whose stories to Ruth concern women whom he has struck. All characters employ verbal violence upon each other. Max employs physical violence as well; with his walking stick he hits Joey in the stomach and Sam across the head. Equating manhood with murder, Max taunts Sam, when the latter declares he fought in the war, "Who did you kill?" When Sam collapses, only apparently dead, Max exclaims, "He's not even dead!"—as if to live signified effeminacy. In harmony with such behavior, Pinter employs animal imagery to describe his characters. Max calls several characters bitches; Lenny calls him a dog cook whose meals are fit for dogs; Max calls Sam a maggot; and at the end of the play he prophesies that Ruth will make animals of them.

Mockery is at first comic, then no longer comic. In act 1, Sam and Max taunt each other about fornication in Sam's car; in act 2, Sam accuses Max's wife and best friend of having committed adultery in that car. The comedy of Max's first-act suggestion that Sam marry and bring his bride to live in the house, where she will service the entire family, is denied in the third-act bargaining concerning Teddy's wife, whom they invite to do the same and more. Max's first, derisively comic comment to Joey—"Who do you think I am, your mother? . . . Go and find yourself a mother."— is echoed noncomically in the final tableau, where Joey, his head in Ruth's lap, may have found her. If one takes boxing as a metaphor for the verbal and psychological fighting among the characters of the play, Max's comic analysis of Joey's deficiencies as a boxer—"What you've got to do is you've got to learn how to defend yourself, and you've got to learn how to attack. That's your only trouble as a boxer. You don't know how to defend yourself, and you don't know how to attack."—suggests Joey's, Lenny's, Sam's, and his own deficiencies in that "game," and Ruth's and probably Teddy's proficiency.

After introducing those who live in the house, Pinter introduces its visitors. The titular homecoming applies to Teddy in the first act, to Ruth in the second. "I was born here," says Teddy in act 1, and Ruth echoes in act 2, "I was born quite near here." Teddy enters the house with a key, which he soon gives Ruth when she leaves for a stroll; this transaction is significant, since the key suggests belonging. Whereas he brings her to his former home in act 1, he leaves her there in act 2. Not only does Teddy's initial action with Ruth hint at the play's conclusion, so does everyone else's. At first, Max does not address her but refers to her as a syphilitic whore; at the end, after she has apparently agreed to become a whore, she does not address him. At first, Lenny inquires whether she might like anything; at the end, she draws up a list of specifications. At first, Joey refuses to comply with Max's command to throw her out; at the end, she pats his head. At first, Sam says nothing to her (he nurses his head, which Max has hit); at the end, he collapses on the floor, where he silently remains for the rest of the play.

Lenny's first encounter with Ruth is a battle for dominance. As they take each other's measure, the comic aspects of their combat are paramount, but these aspects disintegrate in the last act when Ruth's future as dominator or dominated is at stake. In both scenes, Ruth wins. As explained by Peter Hall, director of the first London and New York productions of *The Homecoming*, and of the film, all the characters "are trying to destroy each other by mockery. The [rule] of the game, though, is that when you are putting somebody on, you must not let the other person know that you are doing it." Though very cruel, adds Hall, the game may also be very funny.[13] Whereas funniness dominates the first act, it diminishes during the second.

In their initial encounter, Lenny tells Ruth two stories, performances or set pieces that may be analogies to the play within a play. As in the play as a whole, each has a comic aspect, contains violence, and has domination as its main thrust. Familiar with Lenny's tactics, and able to maintain a facade of detachment, Ruth reveals none of the discomfort, shock, or insecurity her storytelling brother-in-law

13. Peter Hall, interview, in the American Film Theatre program of *The Homecoming*.

tries to elicit. "How did you know she was diseased?" asks Ruth, calmly, when Lenny talks of hitting and kicking a syphilitic woman, and when he abruptly changes the subject at the end of the second story—"I just gave her a short-arm jab to the belly and jumped on a bus outside. Excuse me, shall I take this ashtray out of your way?"—she responds calmly, giving no ground, "It's not in my way." Through proficiency at this indirect boxing, Ruth emerges as the dominant party and comically anticipates the play's tragicomic conclusion.

Apparently an effete victim, Teddy emerges relatively unscarred. Beneath the comic exchange between him and Lenny in act 2, hostility is evident. "Eh, Teddy, you haven't told us much about your Doctorship of Philosophy. What do you teach?" "Philosophy." Effectively, Teddy mocks the mocker. When Lenny, questioning his brother about the known and the unknown, insinuates that his brother merits no respect, Teddy maintains his good-humored detachment and gears his response to the superficial aspects of the question rather than to the subtext: "I'm afraid I'm the wrong person to ask." Though Lenny presses, employing pseudo-philosophical locutions, Teddy neither budges nor drops his calm reasonableness.

LENNY: But you're a philosopher. Come on, be frank. What do you make of all this business about being and non-being?
TEDDY: What do you make of it?
LENNY: Well, for instance, take a table. Philosophically speaking. What is it?
TEDDY: A table.
LENNY: Ah. You mean it's nothing but a table. Well, some people would envy your certainty, wouldn't they, Joey? For instance I've got a couple of friends of mine, we often sit round the Ritz having a few liqueurs. . . .

Continuing to embroider and to move around the subject, Lenny dances about the boxing ring, as it were, and looks in vain for an opening. The very language of the two brothers reveals their different techniques and capabilities. Whereas Teddy is direct and effective (his statements are simple and clear), Lenny evades and weakly takes time to reach the point ("Well, I want to ask you something," "Well, look at it this way," "Well, for instance"). Essentially, Teddy in his match with Lenny does what Ruth later suggests: he restricts his observations to precisely what happens. In his own words, he but not Lenny operates "on things and not in things"; he allies, relates, balances, observes, and refuses to permit himself to become lost in them.

His wife Ruth is no less and perhaps more adept in such battles. When the men vie, she—the only woman present—stops their dialogue by stressing the importance of her sex and sexuality. Not that she says so explicitly. Stating the facts of her leg, underwear, and lips, she thereby establishes their sexual value and power. As if visually to suggest the men's acquiescence to such worth and authority, she remains securely seated while the men rise and all but Teddy leave, displaced. After she and Teddy spar, he—also displaced—leaves the room. Until Ruth's statement about her leg, the combat is comic. From that point until Teddy leaves the room, laughter stops.

But it returns, and it remains even during the sexual scenes. As Joey lies upon Ruth, Max tells Teddy how broad-minded he is. Then: *"He peers to see* RUTH's *face under* JOEY, *turns back to* TEDDY," and tells him, "Mind you, she's a lovely girl." Comedy underlies the family's proposal that Ruth become a prostitute for them and Teddy their stateside representative, as it does their mockery of the imperturbable academic, who unflinchingly sets forth his wife's alternatives, remain or leave with him. Every bit as much in control, Ruth refuses to yield to her husband and she coolly prods the other men to raise the ante. The proposal, made partly in jest, as a way to get at Teddy, turns startlingly noncomic when Ruth accepts it as a serious possibility. The family submits to all her demands. When Sam collapses after he blurts out a declaration that Max's wife was unfaithful to him, Ruth calmly comments that while the terms of the business arrangement are attractive, she prefers to finalize it later, and Teddy, looking down at Sam, whose first entrance was a return from the airport, remarks casually, "I was going to ask him to drive me to London airport." Although the family wins Ruth's presence, they fail to break Teddy, who maintains his grip of the situation. When Max, in a farewell handshake, tells his son, "It's been wonderful to see you," Teddy no less affably repeats the phrase. Since he does not submit, this acknowledgment, like the scene it concludes, remains comic.

When Teddy is about to leave, Ruth tells him, as a prostitute would, not to be a stranger. At this point, laughter stops—shockingly and conclusively. The sexual jokes are no longer funny. Having decisively turned tragicomic, the play denies its sources of laughter. Although Teddy leaves intact, the apparently victorious males who remain are acted upon by the sole woman in their midst, who controls them. They have "won" Ruth from her husband, yet this final scene suggests not the ending of comedy, in which love makes everyone content, but the hollow victory of tragicomedy, as the queen bee rules the men in the hive.[14] Whereas act 1 ends as Max asks his son for a cuddle and a kiss, act 2 ends as he asks his daughter-in-law for a kiss, and in neither case is his request granted. In act 1, however, Max's demand for affection suggests an invitation to battle, and a partially comic stalemate results. By contrast, his demand

14. In act 2, Max tells Ruth, who at the end of the play displaces him as head of the household, "you're kin. You're kith. You belong here." The dialogue recalls *A Slight Ache*, where Edward calls the Matchseller, who at the end of the play displaces him as head of the household, "My kith and kin."

in act 2 has nothing comic about it. The final image of the play is not stalemate but Max's defeat at the hands of his daughter-in-law, who remains silent while "*He falls to his knees, whimpers, begins to moan and sob,*" crawls to her, and pleads for affection. When the curtain falls, the disgruntled old man no longer provokes laughter, which has stopped irrevocably. The family of which Max is nominal head reunites with a woman who becomes its actual head, but this reunited family, to which the wandering son may perhaps return from time to time, repudiates the exclusively festive quality associated with the conclusion of comedy. Although Ruth enjoys her triumph, her enjoyment mocks happiness and her triumph sardonically taunts the concept of a happy ending.

Despite his employment of the essential tragicomic form that shapes his other plays, Pinter adapts that form to the distinctive content of *The Homecoming*. In this savage play, whose violence is verbal as well as physical, comedy too is savage, for the characters—sometimes explicitly, sometimes implicitly—taunt each other. While their mockery amuses the spectator, its underlying destructiveness also shocks him. From the very beginning, the play elicits both amusement and shock. As the characters battle for dominance over each other, laughter accompanies their maneuvers and the cessation of laughter accompanies the climaxes of these encounters, particularly the victories. Although shock does not invariably accompany amusement in this play, it frequently does, and it does so increasingly as the play progresses. To change Shaw's image of the spectator of modern tragicomedy, the spectator of *The Homecoming* frequently laughs with one side of his mouth and gasps with the other—until the shocks of this tragicomedy make laughter impossible and leave him gasping with both sides of his mouth.

Tea Party (produced 1965)

Whereas the reference to "teatime" serves as a prelude to sexual activity *à deux* in *The Lover*, the titular scene of *Tea Party* incorporates such activity *à trois*. The play's opening scene suggests a sexual comedy about husband, wife, and secretary. In the first scene, Disson hires Wendy as his "very private secretary." She crosses, uncrosses, and recrosses her legs in a manner perceived by the audience as sexy, and she admits she left her previous employer because "he never stopped touching me," an explanation that prompts Disson's comically unexpected question, "Where?" Later in the play, Disson's wife, also a secretary in her husband's firm, considers that employers "might not want to touch me in the way they wanted to touch her." Sexuality is a source of verbal comedy, as in the double entendre that ends the dictation scene, when Wendy reads from her pad, "There should be no difficulty in meeting your requirements."

But the end of the play denies comedy. At the play's start, Disson acquires a secretary and a wife (as well as a brother-in-law, whom he meets the same day he hires the secretary), and the denial of comedy does not come about because Disson loses either woman, it comes about even though he keeps both. What begins as a comedy about a cock-of-the-walk, a successful, self-made businessman who hires, acquires, and commands, ends with his abilities undercut. Unable to see or command, at the mercy in business and personal life of the other three figures, he perceives or imagines sexual as well as business links among them. At the start, Disson stands. At the end, he sits; then, still in his chair ("Anyone would think he was chained to it!" exclaims his brother-in-law), he falls to the floor. Even Disson's diction in the first scene ironically forecasts his end: "I've had a look," "You've heard," "I see." At the end of the play, his wife asks him, "Can you hear me? . . . Robert, can you see me?" Disson does not progress from having all to losing all, which might be a tragic movement. His loss may exist in his imagination rather than in reality, and his wife's solicitude may be perfectly sincere.

So *Tea Party* progresses, and the play's end denies the exclusiveness of the comedy that inheres in its early scenes. Reflecting Disson's deterioration are analogues of the play within a play, the amusing eulogies delivered by Disson's brother-in-law, Willy, who first praises his sister:

> My mother and I would, upon entering the music room, gaze in silence at Diana's long fingers moving in exquisite motion on the keys. As for our father, our father knew no pleasure keener than watching his daughter at her needlework. A man whose business was the State's, a man eternally active, his one great solace from the busy world would be to sit for hours on end at a time watching his beloved daughter ply her needle.

This description of Diana's father may fairly describe her husband, who at the unamusing end of the play sits for hours on end as he silently watches, perhaps in his imagination, his beloved Diana's exquisite motion as she engages in sexual activity with her brother and Wendy. In response to the eulogy, Diana affectionately kisses her brother, whereas at the end of the play, as perceived by her husband, she warmly responds to his sexual caresses. Willy's second and funnier eulogy, purportedly of the groom, changes from praise of Disson to praise of Diana. As it does so, it hints at Disson's diminished position later in the play. "I have not known Robert for a long time," says Willy, who met him the previous day. His sister, he declares, equals or surpasses her husband in integrity, and in swimming, he continues with a non sequitur, she can probably beat him in the two-hundred-meter breast stroke. Diana responds as to the first eulogy. These comic performances within the play anticipate the play's noncomic conclusion, for both—particularly the second—undercut Disson's stature as they strengthen Diana's.

Disson's pride during the early part of the play amuses because it resembles brag; excessive pride in the manufacture of bidets, a far cry from heroic accomplishment, suggests an absence of realistic perspective and the self-deception characteristic of comedy. His comically pompous description of the sort of person he dislikes anticipates what he becomes:

> I don't like dithering. I don't like indulgence. I don't like self-doubt. I don't like fuzziness. I like clarity. . . . A man's job is to assess his powers coolly and correctly and equally the powers of others. Having done this, he can proceed to establish a balanced and reasonable relationship with his fellows. In my view, living is a matter of active and willing participation. . . . Nothing is more sterile or lamentable than the man content to live within himself. . . . It seems to me essential that we cultivate the ability to operate lucidly upon our problems and therefore be in a position to solve them. . . . Everything has a function.

Later in the play, Disson dithers and, because of his failing vision, must be indulged. He becomes possessed by self-doubt, has fuzzy and unclear perception, and fails to assess correctly either his powers or those of others. Unable to have a balanced and reasonable relationship with others, he stops active participation in life, lives within himself, and is unable to operate lucidly (an ironically apt adverb) upon his problems or to solve them. He ceases to function entirely.

Laughter begins to erode when Disson's eyesight begins to deteriorate. When he gropes under the table for a Ping-Pong ball, laughter stops. Appropriately, it begins again when his eye examination reveals his eyesight to be uncommonly good. Laughter stops suddenly once more, however, when Disson almost severs his son's fingers with a saw (does Pinter purposely pun?). A balance of laughter and tension pervades the scene wherein Wendy ties her chiffon scarf around Disson's eyes—comic as the blindfolded employer touches his secretary while she is on the phone ("Oh, I will. Of course I will," she tells the caller, in one of several comic double entendres), becoming less comic when the blindfolded man overhears what he thinks is sexual activity between Wendy and Willy in the adjoining office, turning comic once more when on his knees he encounters his wife, then less comic at the suggestion that Diana was in the other room in a sexual triad, and less comic still when one realizes that the sexual triad may have existed only in Disson's imagination.

As Disson's sight continues to diminish, so does laughter. Though Wendy at one point teases him with "being naughty again," for she thinks he is playing a sexual game when he says he is unable to see her, the comedy that this sexual game previously established is quickly denied by the reality of blindness. Although comedy returns, particularly in the verbal exchanges between Disson and his parents, the metaphor of sight gives that comedy a noncomic edge: "Have I seen that mirror before?" asks Disson's mother. "No. It's new." "I knew I hadn't seen it." When the tea party shifts to Disson's perspective, however, and he imagines sex play among wife, brother-in-law, and secretary, laughter ends. Because his eyes are bandaged, what he sees probably exists only in his imagination. When the bandage is removed, he stares unseeing, and he gives no evidence that he hears his wife's solicitous words.

Tea Party focuses upon sense and sensuality. Initially, and as the play develops, both are sources of much of its comedy. When the protagonist actually loses his sense of sight, though not when he does so in play (with his secretary), laughter stops, as it does when he notices or imagines that the two women in his life engage in sexual activity with another man. At the end of the play, when his loss of sight seems total, and when in his imagination he believes he has also lost both his women, the comic qualities of sense and sensuality are denied.

The Basement (produced 1967)

Like *Tea Party*, the beginning of *The Basement* sets up a triangular sex comedy, whose points are not, as in the former play, one man and two women but rather one woman and two men: the girl, the stud, and the schnook. The basis of such a comedy is the schnook's desire to take the place of the stud. Although this is precisely what happens, the play's end denies the exclusiveness of the comic genre from which it derives, for the rivalry between schnook and stud becomes too bitter and violent, the stud at the end assumes the schnook's role, and the cycle suggested by the last scene intimates that the happy conclusion of the schnook's desires is far from conclusive but rather a temporary stopping place, the initiation of another cycle, in which the same male players will perform each other's roles.

Into the basement flat of Law, whose name indicates order, constraint, and regularity, appears his old friend Stott, whose name, which means a young bull and may suggest stud, connotes virility. Law invites Stott in. Outside in the rain, unseen by the inhabitant of the basement, is the visitor's girl, Jane. The final scene of the play repeats the situation and dialogue of the opening scene, but with the men's positions reversed. Stott's initial reference to Jane is comic, for his offhand allusion to a girl who stands in the rain occurs after two pages of dialogue, and Law's repetitions of Stott's phrases emphasize the comic nature of the situation and of Stott's initial speech: "Oh, by the way, I've a friend outside. Can she come in?" "A friend?" "Outside." "A friend? Outside?" "Can she come in?" "Come in?" Only after Law agrees and Stott goes to the door, is Law finally able to articulate what his previous questions meant, "What's she doing outside?"

Verbally, the contrast between schnook and stud is comic, for while the girl undresses and gets into bed, and the stud turns off the lamps and joins her, the schnook in his role of host accommodatingly inquires, "Can I get you some cocoa? Some hot chocolate?" Visually too, the situation is comic: "*Night.* LAW *lying on the floor, a cushion at his head, covered by a blanket. His eyes are closed. Silence. A long gasp from* JANE. LAW'*s eyes open.*"

When romance between schnook and girl arises, the situation remains comic, for in a reversal of conventional roles, Jane makes advances to Law. She caresses him, whispers to him, and urges him not to resist her, while he primly and nervously refuses to yield. Comedy persists when rivalry develops. After permitting Law to assume the role of masterful host at a bar, and to repeat "same again" five times, Stott calmly undercuts him: "I'll change to Campari." Nor does the comedy cease when Stott, without being explicit, suggests that he understands the new, sexual relationship between Jane and Law. Stott reminisces about Law's skill at squash tennis.

> STOTT: Your style was deceptive.
> LAW: It still is.
>   LAW *laughs.*
>   It still is.
> STOTT: Not any longer.

The laughter stops briefly when Stott's sudden refusal to race makes Law fall and hit his chin on the ground, but it returns when Stott, condescendingly but politely patting Law's shoulder, frustrates his host's efforts to evict him. Even Stott's efforts to make love to Jane while he orders Law to find a Debussy record create a funny scene, for Law flings record after record at the wall until he finds it.

When Jane decisively rejects Stott—she moves away from him when he tries to touch her breast—laughter stops and the play denies its exclusively comic expectations. The subsequent violence is no longer playful, Jane's promptings to Law become more urgent and insistent, Law attempts to betray Jane, and when Stott becomes ill, Jane and Law hope he will die. After Stott's recovery, the rivalry becomes violent: Stott hurls a bowl of fruit across the room, he rolls large marbles at Law, who defends himself with a flute—an ineffectual cricket bat in a dangerous game against an opponent whose play is far from playful. As the game's savagery intensifies, Stott bowls a large marble that hits Law on the knee, then another that crashes into Law's forehead and fells him. Next, they face each other, in more dangerous battle, with broken milk bottles. But Pinter is not simple or schematic, even in this play whose progress is more rather than less schematic than his plays usually are, for the denied laughter returns briefly as, in contrast to Stott and Law, who employ broken milk bottles as deadly weapons, Jane pours milk from a bottle into a jug, then from the jug into cups, then stirs the cups—in strikingly funny counterpoint to the men's dangerous confrontation. But the scene sharply closes with a firm denial of the brief comedy: in a sudden thrust, the broken milk bottles smash together.

In the final scene, which repeats the opening scene, schnook and stud have exchanged roles. In his basement flat, Stott welcomes a visitor, Law, and invites him in, while unseen by Stott, Jane stands outside. The second time around, however, the scene is not funny, for the spectators are aware of the consequences of the men's words and actions. This final scene is not the conclusive, happy ending of a comedy. Nor, for that matter, does it finalize the situation of a triangular sex comedy. Rather, it depicts a temporary stage in an ever-recurring cycle, as tragicomic as the fate of Sisyphus, though unlike Sisyphus, Pinter's schnook temporarily tastes the fruit and drinks the water that at other stages were not his.

Old Times (produced 1971)

The beginning of *Old Times* is comic, the end a denial of that comedy's exclusiveness. At the beginning of the play, Deeley smiles and chuckles; at its end, he cries. Established at the start is a comedy based on happy memories about the past. As the play continues, memories arouse rivalry and a battle for domination of a person through participation in or ownership of her past. In the first scene, comedy derives from theft of a possession (according to Kate, Anna stole her underwear). Kate refers to Anna's attempted appropriation of her smile. Pinter dramatizes Anna's usurpation of Deeley's memories and Deeley's appropriation of Anna's words. The husband and the wife's friend vie for control of the wife. Since knowledge means power, memory is their weapon. From the initial references to Anna literally getting into Kate's pants, through Deeley's recollection of lesbians who masturbate in a movie house, through discussions of who should dry Kate when she emerges from her bath, to Deeley's hints (prompted more, perhaps, by his insecurity and imagination than by actuality) that Kate and Anna are or were lesbians, sexuality underlies much of the play. But the subject of sex, often very funny, particularly at the play's start, is no longer humorous at the play's end. Though husband and wife reunite at the close of *Old Times*, their reunion denies happiness, for it involves capitulation and defeat, and whereas the start of the play recalls pleasure and sharing, the play's conclusion suggests desolation, domination, and what may be a death in life.

At the beginning of the play, characters attempt to pin down the past—Anna's size and complexion, the nature of her friendship—whereas at the end, when Kate pins down the past precisely by recalling Anna as dead, comedy departs. From the outset, Pinter emphasizes the uncertainty of memory. Is Anna thin or fat? Says Kate, "Fuller than me. I think." "I suggest," Pinter said in 1964, "there can be no hard distinction between what is real and what is unreal, nor between what is true and false."[15] In 1971 he indicated, as partial reason, "So much is imagined and that imagining is as true as real," and he admitted that one of Anna's statements is a key line in the play: "There are some things one remembers even though they may never have happened. There are things I remember which may never have happened but as I recall them so they take place."[16] By giving events or recollections of such events validity, they are created and shared in the present. The old times may or may not have occurred, but actions based on discussions of them do occur. Part of the impact of the opening scene derives from the vivification of memory. As Kate recalls Anna, she creates her, and—physically present during the conversation about her, in dim light, with her back to Kate and Deeley (and the audience)—Anna turns, coming to life, at the end of their discussion about her. But whereas discussion of the past recreates life at the start of the play, which is appropriate to comedy, discussion of the past at the conclusion of *Old Times* creates death, last rites, and the spattering of dirt on a face, suggestive of burial—all of which are appropriate to that final denial of the exclusiveness of comedy that is a hallmark of modern tragicomedy. Although dim light opens the play, whose first word (a reference to Anna's complexion) is "dark," the play's beginning is comic. Although the play ends in a blaze of bright light, brought up

15. Harold Pinter, "Writing for the Theatre," *Evergreen Review* 8 (August–September 1964): 80.
16. Mel Gussow, "A Conversation (Pause) with Harold Pinter," *The New York Times Magazine* (December 5, 1971): 43.

sharply to the lightning instruments' highest reading, that end denies comic brightness and spotlights desolation.

Battles that are comic in the early part of the play turn noncomic at the end. The memory of Kate becomes for Anna and Deeley a method to exclude the other, who does not share it. Unclear until later in the play is the fact that the person who is the source of contention may, because she is the sought-after prize, control the seekers, as Ruth does in *The Homecoming*. As Anna and Deeley vie for Kate, they transform her from a person into an object, and thus demean her. "You have a wonderful casserole," says Anna with a slip of the tongue. "I mean wife. So sorry." Whereas Anna comically transforms Kate into a thing early in act 1, Kate noncomically makes Anna a corpse at the end of act 2. In Kate's presence, Deeley refers to her in the third person, and though these references are comic in context, they imply her helpless dependence upon him. At the end of act 2, she reduces him to helpless dependence on her. He talks of holding her face in his hands, then removing his hands and letting it float away. Though the image debases, it is at least tender and associated with life-giving water. At the end, Kate talks of throwing dirt upon his face—a phrase whose funereal associations are more damaging.

Comically, Deeley and Anna contend. In act 1, he tries to denigrate her by degrading her words (first "lest," then "gaze"), for by suggesting they are old-fashioned ("Haven't heard it for a long time," he says of the first, "Don't hear it very often" of the second), he implies she is old. In act 2, he attempts to usurp her position by appropriating the latter word. More cleverly and less comically, Anna tries to appropriate his memory of seeing the film *Odd Man Out*.

Shortly after Deeley's second attempt to demean Anna's vocabulary, their contest surfaces significantly as they sing popular songs. He sings the opening lines of "Lovely To Look At" and "Blue Moon," suggesting it is he rather than she who really knows the lovely and delightful Kate, and that Kate, who like the blue moon stood alone, was unattached when he first saw her. Beginning the next round, Anna changes to "They Can't Take That Away From Me," the appropriateness of which is obvious. Although she sings the song's first line, Deeley interrupts with the stanza's concluding, titular line. Switching songs again, Anna begins "The Way You Look Tonight," which suggests that Kate may look lovely for *her* sake. Interrupting assertively, as if to repossess his wife, Deeley sings that he has a woman crazy for him. Although Anna begins another obviously appropriate song, it is Deeley who, concluding the stanza, implies that all the things Kate is, are his rather than Anna's. The contest continues. Anna begins to sing "I Get A Kick Out Of You," but it is Deeley who, singing the final, titular line, suggests that the kicks are his. Not to be outmaneuvered, Anna throws smoke in Deeley's eyes when she sings that *her* true love has been true, for something inside her cannot be denied. As is his wont, Deeley interrupts, but since Anna completes the song, smoke once more gets in Deeley's eyes. In stichomythic fashion, each sings a line of "These Foolish Things Remind Me of You," but neither concludes the song. This song-contest, a performance, is an analogue of the play within a play, observed onstage by Kate and self-consciously performed by the singers. Encapsulating their rivalry over possession of Kate, the comic medley of songs of love, possession, and memory in this first act ends inconclusively.

In what amounts to a second-act reprise, Kate and Deeley again engage in a singing-within-a-play duel, but in act 2 they only sing one song, whose subject is possession: "They Can't Take That Away From Me." Whereas they sang two lines of it in act 1, they now go through two stanzas, each of which ends with the title, and each time Deeley sings it, asserting thereby that what he has cannot be taken from him. As a play within a play suggests the frame play, so do these songs within a play suggest the comedy, rivalry, ferocity of combat, and conclusion of *Old Times*,[17] in which Anna fails to take Kate away from Deeley.

The play's first monologue of memory is Anna's—her first words, in fact—and while its tone is lightly comic, the recollection of the frenetic activity of Kate's former life in London becomes a slightly threatening contrast to the quiet of her present life by the sea. Deeley seems to sense the threat: "*Slight pause*," then, "We rarely get to London." The second memory monologue is Deeley's, concerning his and Kate's meeting after a showing of *Odd Man Out* in a run-down neighborhood theater.[18] Though affectionate as

17. Curiously, a song Deeley and Anna do *not* sing is one whose title, "Seems Like Old Times," incorporates the title of Pinter's play and whose lyrics (by John Jacob Loeb, music by Carmen Lombardo) harmonize with this play. As in the song, Pinter's characters, repeating old times, have a dinner date, talk with each other, and stay up for hours. To Anna and Kate, being with each other once more seems like old times. Although the three characters do not do things they used to do, as in the song, they discuss those things. As they recall past events, the old times, or what they remember them to have been, take place. *Seems* like old times? In a sense it does, for the present does not entirely recapture the past. In another sense, however, the three characters of this play know not seems, for their imagining of old times makes them so. Although wariness is appropriate when one tries to interpret a play not by dialogue it contains but by dialogue it does not contain, the words of this particular song are apt and they supplement rather than replace interpretation based on dialogue in the play. A sound reason for having omitted this song, if Pinter purposely did so, is that its inclusion would have been too obvious.

18. The monologue is perceptively analyzed in Arthur Ganz, "Mixing Memory and Desire: Pinter's Vision in *Landscape, Silence,* and *Old Times,*" in *Pinter,* edited by Ganz (Englewood Cliffs, N.J.: Prentice-Hall, 1972), pp. 171–73 and Stephen Martineau, "Pinter's *Old Times*: The Memory Game," *Modern Drama* 16 (December 1973): 288–89.

well as funny, the tale undermines affection and laughter, for its reductive and degrading references and associations reflect contemptuously upon Kate. Deeley met her in "a fleapit" that had lesbian usherettes, he refers to her as "a trueblue pickup," and his recollection of their meeting evokes a memory of a childhood toy (perhaps his phrase "only tricycle" consciously echoes her reference to her "only friend"). Moreover, he places at the top of his hierarchy, the person for whom "even now" he would commit murder, not his wife but Robert Newton, who acted in *Odd Man Out*. While the speech is funny, the exclusiveness of the comedy is undercut by Deeley's demeaning terms. Still, a comic and affectionate spirit dominates, for following the story he dispossesses the movie actor from the top of the hierarchy: "I thought she was even more fantastic than Robert Newton." The resonances of *Odd Man Out* continue in the second act, where Deeley recalls a man named Luke (Newton played Lukey in the film); and the Robert Newton episode in the film oddly hints at the play's ending, for in *Odd Man Out* Newton plays a mad artist who wants to capture on canvas the look of death in the eyes of an I.R.A. gunman on the run, played by James Mason, who dies at the end of the film.

Although the first act is mostly comic, several aspects foreshadow a tragicomic conclusion. Anna's remembrance of the crying man who lay across Kate's lap anticipates and perhaps helps create Deeley's enactment of that scene at the end of the play. While Deeley's comments on the story evoke laughter in the first act ("He went twice and came once," and after a pause, "Well, what an exciting story that was"), his enactment at the close of the play freezes the memory of that laughter. Kate's accusation that Anna discusses her as if she were dead anticipates her revenge in the final scene when she deanimates Anna.

Anna usurps part of Deeley's past which excludes her,

and transforms Deeley into an odd man whom she thrusts out, when she recalls that she and Kate saw *Odd Man Out*, an unexpected memory that interrupts comic dialogue about Kate's lack of recklessness. Ineffectively, and comic partly because of his ineffectuality, Deeley attempts to assume the posture of sophisticated traveller that he had associated with Anna and her husband, and to mock her as he does so. Does Deeley lie, as Albert lies in *A Night Out*, when he says he works in films? Deeley concludes a description of his cinematic activities with the assertion, "I wrote the film and directed it. My name is Orson Welles." His statement is a quotation of Welles's spoken credits at the close of *The Magnificent Ambersons* (a suggestion that Deeley apes film makers but may not be one himself). This film, which like *Old Times* contains characters who remember old times and includes a modified repetition of past action, was butchered by studio executives more powerful than Welles (a possible suggestion of Deeley's powerlessness). More important, however, is the simple fact that Deeley makes the statement: by his overly inisistent assertions about his sophistication, abilities, and professional esteem, he resembles the Player Queen who protests too much. His repetition of a phrase denies the factual nature the phrase insists on: "As a matter of fact I am at the top of my profession, as a matter of fact." Maintaining he is like members of Anna's circle, he implies he is sufficiently above such people to be contemptuous of them, while his words suggest he is really below them. When Deeley declares in a comically contemptuous manner that the "articulate and sensitive people" with whom he (or Anna?) associates are "mainly prostitutes," Kate steps in to change the subject. Excluding him, and stopping the comedy, she allies herself with Anna and behaves as if they were in their London flat, discussing what to do that evening and what men to call. Although she devitalizes Anna more conclusively at the end of the final act, Kate anticipates that conclusion at the end of the first act, when, treating her husband as if he were not present, she deanimates him.

Whereas act 1 is basically comic, act 2 basically denies the exclusiveness of that comedy. Act 1 begins with Deeley and Kate discussing Anna, act 2 with Deeley and Anna discussing Kate. He and Anna had met before, Deeley recalls, at The Wayfarers Tavern, where he alone "had a thigh-kissing view" of her. Attempting to dominate Anna by implying the power of his masculinity, an echo of his "true-blue pickup" tale in the first act, and by hinting at a homosexual relationship between Anna and Kate, an echo of the lesbian usherettes, he recounts his recollection amusingly, then nastily ends the humor of the tale when he reminds Anna that she is now about forty and unlike the alluring woman who attracted him twenty years ago.

After Kate returns, she, not Anna, initiates a return to the together-in-London situation that excludes Deeley, and she refers to men she and Anna knew in those days. With this second rejection of her husband, laughter stops once more, though it returns temporarily and more seriously undercut. Attempting to make firmer the link between herself and Kate, Anna talks directly to Deeley about when she knew his wife, as if she and not he were the authority on Kate. Threatened, Deeley implies that they were lesbians. "Sounds like a perfect marriage," he says of their life together, and he suggests that Anna's statements about the subject are distasteful. Since she has said nothing explicit about a sexual side to their relationship, however, and since he may only have inferred what she in no way implied, he founders when pressed and cannot explain what disturbs him.

Kate shatters the humor that derives from Deeley's statements when after having remained absolutely silent for more than three pages she tells him, "(*Swiftly*) If you don't like it go." At this point, laughter stops decisively.

While the play denies comedy, however, it does not deny compassion, for the bond between husband and wife fails to snap and Kate soon becomes supportive of Deeley. He is sensitive and lovable, she tells him, rather than crass. When Anna attempts to intrude into their relationship, Kate stops her by verbally laying out her corpse. Kate does not submit to Deeley but takes him as a ruler takes a subject, and she does not banish him as she banishes Anna, whom she liquidates in the final words of the play: "He asked me once, at about that time, who had slept in that bed before him. I told him no one. No one at all." Kate destroys Anna. Whereas the action of act 1 is the dispossession of Deeley, the action of act 2 is the dispossession of Anna. Suggesting this reversal is the placement of the furniture, which in act 2 is *in precisely the same relation to each other as the furniture in the first act, but in reversed positions.*

Visually, Pinter bolsters the characters' relationships in the play's last, wordless scene: Anna, alone, lies on the divan, whereas Deeley and Kate are together. The outsider lies as if on a slab, and husband and wife reunite. Yet Anna is not thrust outside, she merely lies apart from the others and is silent. Though Deeley reunites with his wife, he breaks down and cries. Their reunion, the conventional end of comedy, denies its exclusively comic nature, for it mocks happiness. In fact, the play's final pictorial image is not one of reunion. After crying in his wife's lap, Deeley moves to an armchair, where he sits slumped, apart from her and crushed by her. Although the outsider does not evict the husband and is destroyed by the wife, the stage images that follow the last line of dialogue emphasize both reunion and breakdown, a tragicomic ending that denies comedy.

Like *The Homecoming, Old Times* concerns a family that receives a visitor, battles for domination among visitor and members of the family as well as between the latter, and a female member of the family who triumphs over the male.

As in *The Homecoming*, laughter accompanies the strata-gems of the characters in their battles to dominate each other, and the cessation of laughter accompanies climaxes and victories. Paradoxically, however, while *Old Times* is less savage, more comic, and more compassionate than the earlier play, its ending may be more devastating, its rejection of the bases of comedy even more complete.

Monologue (produced 1973)

Whereas *Old Times* concerns two female friends and a man, *Monologue* concerns two male friends and a woman. Initially, *Monologue*—which is a monologue—suggests a comedy based on friendship, sex, and family. At its tragi-comic end, pleasure loses its bloom, for friendship is insisted upon but not affirmed, sex is both fulfilled and denied, and a family remains intact in a way that excludes the father's friend.

At the play's outset, verbal wit derives from friendli-ness: "I think I'll nip down to the games room. Stretch my legs. Have a game of ping pong. What about you? Fancy a game? How would you like a categorical thrashing? I'm willing to accept any challenge, any stakes, any gauntlet you'd care to fling down. What have you done with your gauntlets, by the way? In fact, *while we're at it*, what hap-pened to your motorbike?" The reference to Ping-Pong is funny, for although the game is a good leg-stretcher, one associates it with arm movements. The inappropriate coup-ling, "categorical thrashing," also seems funny, as does the word "gauntlet," which is hardly a term one would employ in connection with a Ping-Pong game, and the reference to gauntlets, as if they were Ping-Pong paddles, is more amus-ing. The final query amuses because it seems to be a non sequitur. At the end of *Monologue*, the speaker's friendliness and affection are undercut by his jealousy and loneliness, and are denied by the listener's silence, which fails to affirm. As the speaker is excluded from his friend's family, which he would not be in a pure comedy, the end of *Monologue* is a tragicomic denial of the exclusiveness of such comedy.

Laughter results from unexpected contrasts—"You looked bold in black. The only thing I didn't like was your face, too white, the face, stuck between your black helmet and your black hair and your black motoring jacket"—and from the conclusion, "you should have had a black face." When at the end of the play the speaker repeats the last phrase, one knows that the person addressed (actually, the empty chair addressed) has had two children by a black woman, whom the speaker wanted, and the phrase is then no longer funny. The speaker's first reference to the black woman is comic, for it is unexpected, though Pinter anticipates with a pun the revelation of the woman's color: "I often had the impression . . . that you two were actually brother and sister . . . an inkling."

While the speaker insists on his durable friendship with both, he reveals, comically, that the two men were rivals, and he comically discloses his jealousy as well: "You're going to say you loved her soul and I loved her body. . . . I know you were much more beautiful than me. . . . But I'll tell you one thing you don't know. She loved my soul." Comedy persists even in the speaker's revelation of thwarted love: "I loved her body. Not that, between ourselves, it's one way or another a thing of any importance. My spasms could be your spasms. Who's to tell or care?"

But when the speaker reveals that he cares, and that she has rejected him because she could both tell and care about the difference, laughter stops. His loss of love and of self-esteem has undermined affection, for which the speaker pleads. Recognizing his own desolation, he acknowledges his envy: "The ones that keep silent are the best off." He knows that the man to whom he speaks feels nothing for him.

Comedy returns when the speaker describes his energy in mathematical terms: "I've got a hundred per cent more energy in me now than when I was twenty two. When I was twenty two I slept twenty four hours a day. And twenty two hours at twenty four. Work it out for yourself." In the very next sentence, however, he insists too much that he is now at his peak, beyond black girls or friends. Still comically, though desperation increases, he also insists he is far beyond cocoa, a refreshment Pinter employs to suggest copulation. In *The Lover*, the sexually active Richard describes his whore as a quick cup of cocoa between trains and in *The Basement*, Law offers a cup of cocoa to Stott, who is then making love to Jane; but the speaker of *Monologue* admits he has left cocoa far behind. With his hollow overinsistence that his tone of voice is ironic and that he is completely free, laughter ends decisively. The freedom he experiences is the freedom that results from utter rejection. From these assertions, it is a few moments to his admission that he loves his friend's children and his plea to become part of that family. He receives no reply. The verbal wit that accompanied apparent self-assurance at the start of the monologue becomes verbal desperation at its end. The friendship apparent at the play's start is undercut at its noncomic end, when the speaker of this tragicomic monologue fails to receive the assurance and acceptance that would be characteristic of comedy. Instead, with thematic and literary appropriateness, the monologist remains alone on stage.

No Man's Land (1974, produced 1975)

With resonances of *The Caretaker* (a seedy visitor who fails to establish himself as a mainstay in the home of a benefactor), *Old Times* (the unreliability of memory), *The Collection* (hints of homosexuality), *The Homecoming* (malicious taunting beneath a veneer of affability), *Tea Party* (self-appraisal that proves inaccurate), and no doubt other works as well, Pinter's most recent play, *No Man's Land*, is an echo chamber of the Pinter canon.[19] It is also an encapsulation of familiar Pinter themes and techniques and an exemplar of Pinter's distinctive tragicomedy.

Established at the start of *No Man's Land* is comedy derived from language, alcohol, and security. The setting's "central feature," as Pinter calls it, embodies wealth and inebriation: "an antique cabinet, with marble top, brass gallery and open shelves, on which stands a great variety of bottles: spirits, aperitifs, beers, etc." One of the two old soakers who are the play's leading characters is a talkative parasite, the other a wealthy writer who has invited him to his home. At the end, the comedy is no longer comic, for the seedy talker (also a writer, apparently) has failed to ingratiate himself with his host, who is a willing prisoner of aides he employs to protect him from outside encroachment. Comically, the opening of the play anticipates a tragicomic conclusion that denies the exclusiveness of that comedy. The play begins as an expensively dressed old man pours whisky into a glass, and within the first seven pages he consumes four glasses of vodka. His boast, "I drink with dignity," proves only partly accurate. He drinks, but not with dignity; he guzzles whisky from the bottle, and three times in the first act he drunkenly falls to the floor. After his and the play's final line, "I'll drink to that," he does so. The opening words signal the outcome. "As it is?" asks Hirst,

19. Pinter even echoes a joke he had employed in *A Slight Ache*: "You are clearly a reticent man." the loquacious Spooner tells the laconic Hirst in the opening scene of *No Man's Land*. In the earlier play, the loquacious Edward calls the silent Matchseller "a little . . . reticent."

referring to unadulterated whisky, as it comes from the bottle. "As it is," affirms Spooner, "yes please, absolutely as it is." Although the concluding lines do not repeat the phrase, they echo it, for Hirst drinks to an unchanging condition, a way of life that will remain as it is, absolutely.

While Spooner's early talkativeness is a source of laughter, the dramatic action either denies or else ironically confirms his statements. He claims he is not one whose expertise and calculated posture provide the persuasive illusion of strength without the actuality, but rather one whose intelligence and perception enable him to puncture the posture and reveal "the essential flabbiness of the stance." However, the comic flabbiness and calculated posture of his utterance hint that the reverse is true. And his comic reiteration of which of the two types he is—"One of the latter, yes, a man of intelligence and perception. Not one of the former, oh no, not at all. By no means."—not only suggests false overprotestation but the proliferation of negatives tends to negate his denials. When the end of the play reveals him to be one of the former, the revelation pitifully erodes the comic. Although Hirst first enjoys the loquacity of Spooner, who in the play's opening and closing scenes does most of the talking, he later does not. Whereas early in the play Spooner's insistence that he takes comfort in the indifference shown him by others, who do not wish him to remain with them for long, is comic in its unexpected inversion of the usual sentiment, Spooner late in the play receives no comfort when Hirst, indifferent to his pleas, refuses to invite him to stay. Tragicomically, Spooner obtains what he claims he wants, but what he gets provides neither pleasure nor comfort. Early in the play, Spooner quotes "a wit" who once called him "a betwixt twig peeper." Comic, for the phrase is a clumsy attempt at cleverness, it is not as "infelicitous" as Spooner agrees it is, for Spooner is a perennial outsider who observes but does not participate in the comradely activities of others. When at the end of the play Hirst rejects Spooner, who remains "a betwixt twig peeper," his fate is not amusing.

Funny during the first part of the play, the subject of Hirst's hospitality is no longer funny during the last. Comic in its hyperbole, Spooner's reference to Hirst's hospitality also raises the subject of the unchanging: "May I say how very kind it was of you to ask me in? In fact, you are kindness itself, probably always are kindness itself, now and in England and in Hampstead and for all eternity." At the end of the play, Hirst ends his hospitality and rejects Spooner "once and for all and for the last time forever," as Foster puts it. The iciness of Foster's "for the last time forever," which Hirst accepts, denies the genial warmth of Spooner's earlier "for all eternity."

The unreliability of memory is funny. In act 1, Spooner recalls a meeting years ago with a former member of Hungarian aristocracy.

HIRST: What did he say?
SPOONER *stares at him.*
SPOONER: You expect me to remember what he said?
HIRST: No.

Later memories of sexual betrayals are also comic. Verbal repetition increases the comic aspects of the relationship between Spooner and Hirst. "And I wonder at you, now," says Spooner, "as once I wondered at him. But will I wonder at you tomorrow, I wonder, as I still wonder at him today?" Equally important, their relationship becomes indefinite and unpredictable. Mockery underlies some of the mnemonic dialogue between them. Like Teddy and Ruth in *The Homecoming*, each understands taunting or malicious undertones, and each coolly, with superficially good humor, can parry such subtle thrusts:

SPOONER: I looked up once into my mother's face. What I saw there was nothing less than pure malevolence. . . . You will want to know what I had done to provoke such hatred in my own mother.

HIRST: You'd pissed yourself.

SPOONER: Quite right. How old do you think I was at the time?

HIRST: Twenty eight.

SPOONER: Quite right.

Later in act 1, their dialogue about memories becomes more overtly cruel. "Tell me more about the quaint little perversions of your life and times," Spooner tells Hirst, and each suggests that the other man's wife left him. When the drunken Hirst ineffectually throws a glass at Spooner, the latter affably asks, "Do I detect a touch of the hostile?" Their derision is still essentially comic. "Remember this," taunts Spooner with rhythm and rhyme, "You've lost your wife of hazel hue, you've lost her and what can you do, she will no more come back to you, with a tillifola tillifola tillifoladi-foladi-foloo." Bleary-eyed with drink, Hirst staggers across the room, falls, rises, falls again, and crawls out the door—still comic, for Spooner silently, without moving or attempting to help, watches him, then lightly comments, again with rhyme, "I have known this before. The exit through the door, by way of belly and floor." At the end of the play, these subjects, no longer broached in comic jingles, are no longer funny. Hostility is no longer comic and mockery is directed toward Spooner, who is verbally expelled.

A threat to Spooner is established with the appearance of Foster and Briggs, who stand between him and Hirst. Yet their encounter is polite, even comic. Indicative of their relationship are their stories, descriptive set-pieces recited for an onstage audience, analogues of the play within a play, like Lenny's stories in *The Homecoming*. Whereas Spooner begins as speaker, he ends as listener. The cumulative effect of these stories, like that of the entire play, is toward greater danger to him. Spooner's act 1 story concerns joy and comradeship, based in part on a visitor from another realm (a fish, appropriately out of water and ominously dead). Since, as Foster admits, he is baffled, Spooner is in a commanding position. But while Foster and Briggs seem, like the fish, out of their element, it soon becomes clear that it is Spooner who is out of his. Foster's story, also in act 1, about an "old stinking tramp" who asked him for money, suggests the old Spooner, who wears *"a very old and shabby suit,"* and it concludes with the old man's departure. Implicitly, Foster suggests that Spooner leave, but at this stage of the action, with Spooner unaware of the extent of his vulnerability, and also uncertain of the precise relationship between the two younger men and Hirst (homosexuality is hinted at, and in the original London production Foster, "a vagabond cock" as Briggs calls him, was obviously homosexual), he is able to parry the verbal thrusts. In the second act, the more overtly brutal Briggs tells Spooner a tale whose hilarity derives from intricate directions he once gave Foster on how to get from one place to another, but the fearful laces the comic, since Briggs demonstrates his own knowledge and expertise, Spooner's confusion and inability to reach the truth of the matter (Foster, says Briggs at the start and close of the story, will deny it), and at certain points Briggs may address Spooner in the present while he quotes himself speaking to Foster in the past ("forget the whole idea. . . . This trip you've got in mind, drop it, it could prove fatal"). Emphasized by and in the story are two points not lost on Spooner: that Briggs and Foster constitute a solidly defensive bulwark against the newcomer Spooner and that Briggs, with a threat, advises a man not to go where he wishes to go.

Though still comic, the final portion of act 1 not only turns more menacing and less comic, it strongly hints at the play's noncomic end. When Hirst returns, Pinter comically suggests the unchanging world that Hirst, rejecting Spooner, will choose at the play's end:

HIRST: ... What day is it? What's the time? Is it still night?
BRIGGS: Yes.
HIRST: The same night?

Significantly, he fails to recognize Spooner, whom Foster explicitly commands, "Bugger off." The comic diminishes. Briggs suggests that Spooner be castrated. Foster warns, "Don't try to drive a wedge into a happy household. You understand me?" In a striking first-act curtain, which anticipates Spooner's rejection at the end of the play, Foster, alone with Spooner, says:

Listen. You know what it's like when you're in a room with the light on and then suddenly the light goes out? I'll show you. It's like this.
He turns the light out.
   BLACKOUT

As the act ends, Foster deprives Spooner, who understands little of the relationship among the three residents of Hirst's home, of the security of light.

Despite the certitude with which Spooner and Hirst in act 2 discuss their past relationship with each other, Pinter tantalizingly calls into question whether they knew each other at all. Upon his entrance in act 2, Hirst greets Spooner as Charles. Later, he refers to him as Charles Wetherby, but the surname may be merely a slip of the tongue, for earlier in this act he called Briggs "Denson" and then failed to contradict or even comment when Spooner referred to "Emily Spooner, my own wife." Although their reminiscences are often hilarious ("Did you have a good war?" asks Hirst), a somewhat taunting quality seems to underlie lapses which may be purposeful and replies which may be only superficially good humored ("The RAF?" "The Navy." "How splendid. Destroyers?" "Torpedo boats." "First rate."). Even the more overtly venomous portions of their mnemonic exchange are comic, such as Hirst's confession that he seduced Spooner's wife, Spooner's that he informed on Hirst to the brother of a girl he had seduced ("What business was it of his?" asks Hirst. "He was her brother," Spooner replies. "That's my point."), Spooner's admission that a girl of whom Hirst was fond practiced fellatio with him, and Spooner's charge that Hirst was active with members of both sexes. Even Hirst's responses are funny: "I'll have you horsewhipped!" and after crying, "This is outrageous!" he calls for a whisky and soda. The comic recriminations and uncomic venom dissolve in alcohol, then in laughter, as Hirst rhetorically inquires, "Where is the moral ardour that sustained you once? Gone down the hatch. (BRIGGS *enters, pours whisky and soda, gives it to* HIRST. HIRST *looks at it.*) Down the hatch. Right down the hatch. (*He drinks.*)"

With the return of Briggs and Foster, comedy decreases, rivalry intensifies. When Spooner asks Hirst to take him on as secretary, and to displace Foster, whom he advises to travel, Spooner makes explicit an objective that had been implicit—a miscalculation, since Hirst, the desperate outsider fails to recognize, seeks to avoid explicit conflict and direct confrontation. Spooner also miscalculates when he offers Hirst, who prefers sequestration to public appearance, a poetry reading in a cheap tavern under his sponsorship—thus further undercutting his position. Spooner's comic garrulousness is less comic, and to Hirst his loquacity suggests "a big fly . . . buzzing." Foster and Briggs do not need to employ physical violence against Spooner. Their verbal violence suggests the physical violence at their disposal. When Hirst reminds his two servants, "We three, never forget, are the oldest of friends," and proposes a toast to their good fortune, he implicitly rejects Spooner. Because the rejection is still implicit, some laughter remains.

But after Spooner's monologue of more than two pages, when the three residents close ranks against the outsider, laughter ceases. Upon Hirst's insistence that the subject be changed for the last time, laughter stops for the last time. No longer will Hirst even hear of Spooner's replacement of Foster. As Foster pointedly interprets his employer, "the subject is changed once and for all. . . . The previous subject is closed. . . . It's forgotten." The present subject is the impossibility of again changing the subject. For the last time, for the rest of time, in perpetual night, Hirst will sit with Foster and Briggs in what Spooner, acknowledging his rejection and employing the words Hirst had previously used, calls "no man's land. Which never moves, which never changes, which never grows older, but which remains forever, icy and silent." The situation remains, in the play's opening words, "As it is." Entering that anomalous and ambiguous area that is no man's land, the play that had initially promised comedy ends with a denial of the exclusive nature of that comedy. In the final scene, the characters remain true to their names. In a verbally caressing manner, Spooner tries to spoon, to court or woo a potential benefactor; he fails. Hirst elects to remain in his frozen hirst, a barren plot of ground, where he is treated with parental-like care by Foster and guarded as if in a brig by Briggs.[20]

20. Names, like other words and phrases, may of course carry multiple associations which are not mutually exclusive. In a letter to the *Times* (London), June 7, 1971, p. 13. D.A. Cairns perceptively observes "the possibly significant fact that all four characters in the play are named after prominent English cricketers of the late nineteenth and early twentieth centuries. The choice does not appear to have been made at random, since three of them, Hirst, Briggs and Foster . . . [were] left-arm bowlers . . . and the fourth, Spooner, who in the play is an outsider and claims to be a poet, was a bats-

In act 1, Hirst had referred to his dream, in which someone was drowning, and Spooner had insisted, "It was I drowning in your dream." Spooner's effort to insinuate himself into Hirst's life by way of Hirst's dream is comic. At the end of act 2, an echo of this subject freezes the memory of laughter. "I was mistaken," Hirst maintains. "There is nothing in the water. I say to myself, I saw a body, drowning. But I am mistaken. There is nothing there." Spooner's hopes, though dashed, are not tragic, but while they had no chance of fulfillment from the start, the thoroughness of his rejection denies comedy. Although Hirst does as he wishes and his domain remains intact, the result—alcoholism and a virtual prison, servants who are masters of the situation while their master though in their power commands and receives just what he wishes—mocks the happy ending associated with comedy.

The wit provided by Spooner's speech, the geniality by the alcohol, and the security by the friendliness of two old men who appear to have something in common: these characteristics emerge at the beginning of *No Man's Land*. By the end of the play, they dissolve. Spooner's language reveals desperation, alcohol is a means of escape and self-isolation, and the two old men are estranged—one secure only in the sense that a cell or tomb provides security, the other evicted from a haven of food, drink, and companion-

man, known for his elegant stroke-play. May there not be a clue here to the play's structure, if not to its meaning?" Since Pinter is a cricket fan who would surely be familiar with the offensive and defensive goals and tactics of bowlers and batters, and who might very well be familiar with the names of these players, the answer to Cairns's question is no doubt affirmative. This interpretation would seem to support the analysis just offered. However, I think it more appropriate to leave the interpretation of *No Man's Land* as cricket match to an Englishman, who is better equipped than I, an American, to discuss one of his national sports. Let me thank Martin Esslin and Charles A. Carpenter, Jr., each of whom directed me to this letter to the *Times*.

ship. As in Pinter's earlier plays, the tragicomic pattern of *No Man's Land* consists of a denial at the play's end of the exclusiveness of the same comic qualities inherent in its beginning. As the themes of this play recall themes of earlier plays, so do the tragicomic stratagems. As in several of his plays, rejection puts an end to laughter. As in *The Caretaker*, the structure of the first act encapsulates the movement of the entire play, and the noncomic threat to an old man, which closes the first act of each play, anticipates a greater threat to his security at the final curtain, when he is spurned by the owner of the house wherein he hoped he would find refuge. Like *A Slight Ache*, *No Man's Land* moves inexorably to a reversal that might be anticipated. Like *The Homecoming* and *Old Times,* laughter accompanies the maneuvers of characters who contend for positions of power, and laughter ceases during the climaxes of their struggles, as it also does during a character's defeat. More explicitly than *Old Times*, the end of *No Man's Land* destroys enduringly the foundations of its comic qualities. The particular manner in which Pinter dramatizes each theme reflects and embodies that theme, and the variety of manners he employs in *No Man's Land* to dramatize a variety of themes creates a rich texture rather than mere repetition.

*   *   *

From *The Room* to *No Man's Land*, a span of almost twenty years, all but a very few of Pinter's plays are tragicomedies that conform to the cardinal characteristics of modern tragicomedy but carry Pinter's distinctive signature. Associated initially and primarily with comedy, they begin with comic expectations and then move to a point where laughter stops. They deny the exclusiveness of comedy in the very terms they first establish to suggest comedy, they carry no real comfort, and they sardonically mock the order and end of comedy. However, Pinter's tragicomic form is not a simple formula that he applies schematically to each play. Rather, it is a basic structure which he varies skillfully and in a complex manner to harmonize with the themes and requirements of each particular play. His consistent employment of this structure, an organic part of his artistic signature, contributes to the distinctiveness of the Pinter canon.

Bibliographical Note
on Harold Pinter's Plays

Although I have examined various editions of Pinter's plays, quotations in the text are, with one exception, keyed to the American editions. That exception is *Monologue,* which has not yet (April 1976) been published in the United States.

Silently, Pinter has revised the first two books cited below. None of his changes is substantive, however, and none require modification of the point of view expressed in this essay. Unless indicated in footnotes (as earlier and revised versions), all quotations are identical in both editions.

Editions Used

The Birthday Party and The Room: Two Plays. New York: Grove Press, 1961; revised edition, 1968.

The Caretaker and The Dumb Waiter: Two Plays. New York: Grove Press, 1961; revised edition, 1965.

The Homecoming. New York: Grove Press, 1966.

The Lover, Tea Party, The Basement. New York: Grove Press, 1967.

Monologue. London: Covent Garden Press, 1973.

No Man's Land. New York: Grove Press, 1975.

Old Times. New York: Grove Press, 1971.

Three Plays: A Slight Ache, The Collection, The Dwarfs. New York: Grove Press, 1962.